CATHOLICS FOR THE COMMON GOOD

An Eternal Offering

DARYL RUSSELL GRIGSBY

Paulist Press
New York / Mahwah, NJ

Cover image by Eky Studio / Shutterstock.com
Cover and book design by Lynn Else

Library of Congress Cataloging-in-Publication Data
Names: Grigsby, Daryl Russell, 1955- author.
Title: Catholics for the common good: an eternal offering / Daryl Russell Grigsby.
Description: New York; Paulist Press, [2024] | Includes bibliographical references. | Summary: "This book profiles forty-two contemporary Catholics of diverse backgrounds who have contributed to the common good by their lives and works, modeling the Eucharistic Prayer, 'Make of us an eternal offering to you.'"—Provided by publisher.
Identifiers: LCCN 2024010272 (print) | LCCN 2024010273 (ebook) | ISBN 9780809157174 (paperback) | ISBN 9780809188796 (ebook)
Subjects: LCSH: Catholics—Biography. | Common good—Religious aspects—Catholic Church. | Christian sociology—Catholic Church.
Classification: LCC BX4651.3 .G75 2024 (print) | LCC BX4651.3 (ebook) | DDC 282.092/2—dc23/eng/20240711
LC record available at https://lccn.loc.gov/2024010272
LC ebook record available at https://lccn.loc.gov/2024010273

ISBN 978-0-8091-5717-4 (paperback)
ISBN 978-0-8091-8879-6 (e-book)

Published by Paulist Press
997 Macarthur Boulevard
Mahwah, NJ 07430
www.paulistpress.com

Printed and bound in the
United States of America

CATHOLICS FOR THE COMMON GOOD

Dedicated to my parents Russell and Jacqueline,
my wife Leslie, my daughters Lauren and Hillary,
and my grandson Roman Russell;
and to Father Paul Magnano, Archdiocese of Seattle,
who conferred on me the Rite of Confirmation,
All Saints Day, 1998.

May He make of us an eternal offering to You.

Eucharistic Prayer III

CONTENTS

INTRODUCTION

THE TWO-THOUSAND-YEAR HISTORY of the Catholic Church is a legacy of human sinfulness. These sins include inquisitions, unholy alliances with corrupt and violent governments, sexual scandals, blessings upon slavery, colonization and conquest, and many other horrors. Yet, this is not the whole history of the Church. There is another side, one of self-sacrifice, solidarity with the poor, authentic prayerfulness, inclusive spirituality, work for justice, and dedication to peace. This side of the Catholic Church is expressed in the Communion of Saints, Catholic social teaching, and the Eucharist.

In the Apostles' Creed we say, "I believe…in the Communion of Saints." That affirmation confirms that we live among, learn from, and are recipients of the prayers of a body of devoted people from all ages and all around the world. A premise of this book is that the thirty-six profiles here are our companions on the journey. We are not alone. God is with us through the humanity of Jesus and the indwelling of the Holy Spirit. Yet, there is more. "We are surrounded by so great a cloud of witnesses" (Heb 12:1). They are not superhumans or angels; they were all born into the human family, and they found a connection to God that inspires and informs our path.

Catholic social teaching is another foundation of our faith journey. Many of the lives described here have both shaped and been shaped by Catholic social teaching. Often described as "the best kept secret" of the Catholic Church, these teachings are in fact not so secret. They are lived every day by Catholics all over the world. Those presented here are but a small portion of the Catholics that serve every day in prisons, in drug clinics, among LGTBQ people, among gang members, and in other places where love makes a difference. They strive for racial justice and for peace. They live the teachings of *Pacem in Terris, Populorum Progressio, Fratelli Tutti, Evangelii Nuntiandi,* and the other documents that lay out Catholic social teaching. The beneficiaries of their work are those that suffer.

Finally, there is the Eucharist. Every Catholic Mass includes this sacrament. While much is made over the bread and wine becoming the Body of Christ, the meaning of the Eucharist is richer than "transubstantiation." A careful listen to the Eucharistic Prayer enables us to hear that, we, the assembly, together become One through the Blessed Sacrament. As Fr. Ron Rolheiser, OMI, notes in *Bread of Life,* "It is we…who are transubstantiated."[1] Yet there is more. Eucharistic Prayer III petitions, "May he make of us an eternal offering to you." Jesus's sacrifice for us does not end in our forgiveness. We move from estrangement from God to union with God, and from union to an offering of ourselves for the life of the world. How are we "offered"? Jesus demonstrated that God's love for us has no boundaries. In response, we offer ourselves to God in our deeds of mercy, inclusion, and the making of justice and peace. The perspective that the Eucharist is the offering of us to God, and through God, to humanity, is not new. St. Augustine's classic, *The City of God,* notes in book 10, "This is the sacrifice of Christians: we, being many, are one body in Christ. And this also is the sacrifice which the Church continually celebrates in the sacrament of the altar, known to the faithful, in which she teaches that she herself is offered in the offering she makes to God."[2]

Centuries later, section 38 of *Gaudium et Spes*, the Pastoral Constitution on the Church in the Modern World, also reminds us:

> Yet He frees all of them so that by putting aside love of self and bringing all earthly resources into the service of human life they can devote themselves to that future when humanity itself will become an offering accepted by God.

Thus, our vocation, our call, is to be engaged in the divine enterprise whereby all of humanity, indeed, all of creation, is "gathered together as one" in Christ. That is not an abstraction but a reality constructed by our deeds of mercy.

Among those who embody our vocation as an eternal offering are individuals from many areas of life. This call is not restricted to bishops, priests, or consecrated religious. Here we find musicians like Mary Lou Williams, theologians like Monika Hellwig and laypersons like Paul Farmer. Catholics are but a portion of the human beings whose connection to God is demonstrated in their work for others. Their story is our story, and it inspires us to deepen our own calling as an eternal offering. The "foreverness" of our call is confirmed in Psalm 1, where the writer notes, "their…delight is in the law of the Lord.…They are like trees planted by streams of water…and their leaves do not wither" (Ps 1:2–3). This passage, and the lives of these individuals, remind us that the time to do good is not past but remains ahead of us.

A distinguishing feature of this book is the diversity of national origins and racial groups represented. There are Africans, Asians, Europeans, Latin Americans, and North Americans. This diversity underscores one of the Catholic Church's great treasures, a global faith. We are sometimes reminded that the word translated as "catholic" derives from the Greek *kath'holou* means "pertaining to the whole." With that understanding, "catholic" then is more than "universal"; it is also "unity in difference." Thus, the global practitioners of faith bring their unique cultural gifts to our common call to love God and build God's reign on earth.

In many respects, the global nature of the Church has been highlighted during the pandemic. As many gatherings and meetings shifted from in person to online, I had the rich opportunity to join Catholics from around the world. Consequently, I prayed with, listened to, and learned from Catholics in Kenya, Hong Kong, Scotland, Vietnam, Italy, Uganda, Mexico, and elsewhere. I also experienced the rich and diverse faith experiences of Catholics in various parts of the United States and from various ethnic backgrounds.

The scriptures speak often of drawing people from east and west, of being a body with many members, and of gifts freely given to all. During every Eucharist we are reminded of the "Church, spread throughout the world." This book provides a small glimpse into the presence and generosity of God among all peoples. These portraits are not ends in themselves but point the way toward many other people who make real the presence of God in acts of welcome, justice, and peace.

Another feature of this book is the focus on the various vocations of the Church: consecrated religious, laypersons, priests, and bishops. Although the various vocations are identified separately, it is important to know that everyone begins as a layperson. In addition, the "boundaries" are sometimes fluid, with paths that move from layperson to consecrated religious and back to layperson.

The impact of women's leadership and service is evident in the following pages. Fr. Augustus Tolton, the first African American priest in the United States, speaks of the influence on his faith of his mother who liberated him from enslavement. Fr. Hans Küng, the outspoken Catholic priest who met with world leaders on the question of peace, is said to have been profoundly influenced by "those five sisters of his." Theologian Diana Hayes writes powerfully of the faith and perseverance of her mother. Those are but a few examples of women in the Church, the descendants of Apostle Mary Magdalene, whose lives reflect the reality, "I have seen the Lord" (John 20:18).

Also, those profiled are not the only representatives of faith in action. They represent what is good and true about Catholicism, and more importantly, about God. There are so many others whose story needs telling and retelling, many others who should be emulated and celebrated for their witness to the faith, Catholics who work for the common good. In fact, new activists, reformers, educators, teachers, ministers, and servants of God join the ranks every day. So accurate are the words of Jesus, "Very truly, I tell you, the one who believes in me will also do the works that I do and, in fact, will do greater works than these" (John 14:12). Enough of the bankrupt dioceses, intolerance to the spectrum of human sexuality, return to patriarchal ideologies, and allegiance to patriotism, nationalism, and intolerance! God's Spirit lives daily in the works of the pilgrim People of God!

> God makes the Church itself a sacrifice pleasing in his sight by preserving within it the love which his Holy Spirit has poured out. Thus the grace of that spiritual love is always available to us, enabling us to continually offer ourselves to God as a living sacrifice, holy and pleasing to him for ever.
>
> Saint Fulgentius of Ruspe, bishop[3]

PART I

CONSECRATED WOMEN

All religious, therefore, with undiminished faith, with charity toward God and their neighbor, with love for the cross and the hope for future glory, should spread the good news of Christ throughout the whole world.

Decree on the Adaptation and Renewal of Religious Life, *Perfectae Caritatis* (*PC*) 2

The ultimate norm of religious life is the following of Christ set forth in the Gospels.

PC 25

1. SISTER ALOYSIUS, OSP / ANNE MARIE BECRAFT

WHEN ANNE MARIE BECRAFT was born a free Black child in Washington, DC, in 1805, she fit an uncommon demographic profile. Of the approximately twenty thousand residents, one-third were Black, and the vast majority of those were enslaved to a white master. The Becraft family negotiated life aware that most of the people who looked like them were the property of someone else, subject to sale, family separation, rape, beating, or whatever suited the master's desire. Further, African Americans in Washington, DC, lived under draconian conditions, including a requirement that all free Black people were required to possess a certificate signed by three reputable white people that they were of "good character." Failure to produce such a document resulted in the auction block and enslavement.[1]

As the Becraft family sojourned in a slaveowner's city, they found solace in the Catholic faith. Near their home in Georgetown was Holy Trinity Parish, and the Becrafts, like many other African Americans, saw the crucified Jesus as their companion in sorrows, and the resurrected Christ as their Savior and hope for a future of justice.

Anne Marie, like Frederick Douglass, Harriet Jacobs, and others, discovered that the only road to dignity and self-determination was learning to read, write, and count. She attended a school for Black and white children until it was shut down in 1820 for providing integrated education. The school's closure did not dampen her enthusiasm for learning and books. Young Anne Marie searched for knowledge. Over time, she realized that though she was still young, her rare opportunities to learn gave her information she could share with others.

She was a daily witness to her neighbors' suffering. Many were recently freed or had escaped from slavery, and thus had no education. Most masters believed that slaves were incapable of learning or that reading made them unfit for servitude. Realizing she could share her gifts of knowledge with others, fifteen-year-old Anne Marie opened a school for her neighbors in her parents' home on Dumbarton Street.[2] Each day, she taught the neighboring children, spending whatever money she had on books, paper, pencils, and other classroom tools. For eight years, surrounded by the reality of slavery, relentless discrimination, and occasional violence, Anne Marie Becraft gave the world of books and reading to local Black children. With no other educational opportunities available, the Black children of her neighborhood soaked up the chance to learn. While opportunities for Black Americans were limited by racism and discrimination, learning provided a sense of empowerment and self-confidence. One can only imagine the many young lives she touched with her passion both for education and her race.

She named her school Georgetown Academy, and during the eight years of operation, she taught an average of thirty-five students each day. Her work was revolutionary, giving Black children tools for freedom in the capital of slavery and white supremacy. We can only guess the courage, charisma, and skill she brought to the classroom.

In 1827, a Jesuit priest at Holy Trinity Parish embraced Anne Marie's academy as a work of the church and an extension of the Gospel. The parish provided Anne Marie with classroom spaces and resources in the church for her school. She was named head teacher and was able to reach more children from the community. During this time, she transformed her school into the first Catholic day and boarding school for Black girls in the entire nation. The visual of her school cannot be overstated. Her Georgetown Academy was near Georgetown College, where three hundred Blacks were enslaved, and close to the Visitation Convent, home to eighty enslaved African Americans. It is recorded that she often walked her "troop of girls, in procession, to devotions on the sabbath at Holy Trinity Church."[3] This she did in a city where the Catholic hierarchy owned slaves and Black worth was established by white-endorsed certificates of character.

Four years later, in 1831, Anne Marie Becraft heard God's call to consecrated life in a religious order. The Catholic Church in general, and religious orders in particular, were as infected with racism as the rest of American society. In fact, in many cases the church was a forerunner and sustainer of white racism. Therefore, religious orders in America forbade Black members.

From her teaching career and community work, Anne Marie was aware of the Oblate Sisters of Providence, founded in 1828 by Mother Elizabeth Lange. The Oblate Sisters' religious mission was the education of Black girls. Anne Marie Becraft was accepted in the Oblate Sisters, and thus she could fulfill her calling to a life of prayer and the continued education of Black girls. Taking the name Sister Aloysius, OSP, Anne Marie Becraft was the eleventh Black woman to become a member of the Oblate Sisters of Providence.

Religious life did not end discrimination for Sister Aloysius and the other sisters in the congregation. Shannen Dee Williams's *Subversive Habits: Black Catholic Nuns and the Long African-American Freedom Struggle* recounts the disrespect Black nuns suffered both from the Catholic Church and the larger society. Under the circumstances, it is a miracle that Becraft and her sisters remained committed to God when the behavior of bishops, priests, white nuns, and white laypeople was contrary to the Gospel.

Anne Marie's life ended on December 16, 1833, when she died at age twenty-eight of a chronic chest ailment. In her brief time on earth, Anne Marie Becraft transformed the lives and futures of hundreds of Black children, and the children of those children. There are perhaps those alive today whose ancestors were touched by the work of their head teacher, Anne Marie Becraft.

It has recently been discovered that Anne Marie's father, William, was the son of a free Black woman who worked as a housekeeper for Charles Carroll, the cousin of Archbishop John Carroll. The archbishop was the founder of Georgetown College. Anne's father is the natural son of Charles Carroll, thereby making Anne Marie Becraft the granddaughter of Charles Carroll and a relative of the archbishop. Little is known of the Black woman who birthed Anne Marie's father. As Georgetown grapples with its own entanglement with slavery, they have taken steps to acknowledge and remedy their complicity. One such step is to honor Anne Marie Becraft and her dedication to Black uplift through education by naming a university building after her.

Anne Marie Becraft will be remembered as the fifteen-year-old Black girl who lived in slavery's shadow but who through faith and vision improved hundreds of lives. She is also now honored by one of the top Jesuit universities in the nation. Through the descendants of her students and a building bearing her name, the Catholic faith and social commitment of Anne Marie Becraft lives on.

> "[Becraft] is remembered, wherever she was known, as a woman of the rarest sweetness and exaltation of Christian life, graceful and attractive in person

and manners, gifted, well educated, and wholly devoted to doing good," according to an 1870 special report submitted to the U.S. Congress on the "Condition and Improvement of Public Schools in the District of Columbia."[4]

2. SISTER THEA BOWMAN, FSPA

WHAT A MYSTERY, AN AFRICAN American girl in Canton, Mississippi, during the 1940s, surrounded by racist threats and murders, embracing the teachings of St. Francis! Who would expect a girl in the heart of Black Protestant church culture to become the most renowned member of a formerly all-white Catholic order, the Franciscan Sisters of Perpetual Adoration. Nothing in the life and legacy of Beth Bowman of Mississippi follows an "expected" pattern.

At nine years old, Beth Bowman announced to her stunned parents that she wanted to become a Catholic and join the Catholic Church. Black Catholics in rural Mississippi were rare, as most African Americans were devout Baptists. Beth's parents believed strongly in education as a route to dignity and self-respect. Her father, Dr. Theon Bowman, graduated from Meharry Medical College in Nashville, and her mother, Mary Esther (Coleman) Bowman was a teacher. Knowing Mississippi public schools for Blacks were designed for a life of secondary status and servitude, they enrolled Beth in the newly opened Catholic school, Holy Child Jesus Elementary, run by nuns from the Franciscan Sisters of Perpetual Adoration. There Beth was attracted to the joy and prayerfulness of the sisters. She later noted that they were "sharing the Good News in ways that were concrete and real. I was not attracted to the church per se so much as I was attracted to Christian people living real Christian witness."[5]

As she grew, so did her faith, culminating in her decision to become a nun in the Franciscans of Perpetual Adoration. That journey took her to La Crosse, Wisconsin, the

Catholic University of America, and other places where Black religious were as rare as Black Catholics in Mississippi. When she completed her novitiate and was accepted into the community, Beth took the name Sister Thea Bowman, as a tribute to her roots and her father, Theon.

While attending Catholic University of America, Sister Thea had a friend who died by suicide. This event changed the trajectory of her life. Her friend's death called her to a deeper level of human connection. Disturbed that she had missed the verbal and silent warning signs of her friend, Bowman later told interviewer Margaret Walker Alexander that she added a discipline of listening to her life. She would "use her natural empathetic gifts to listen closely to each person...and integrate my natural soul into all my relationships."[6] Everywhere she went, she integrated her Black soul, her human soul, her natural soul, into every encounter.

In predominantly white spaces where Blacks were seldom seen, Sister Thea Bowman proudly displayed the richness of Black spirituality. Through song, fervent prayer, passionate speech, and deeds of justice, she opened many hearts and minds. As a Black nun in the white Franciscan Sisters of Perpetual Adoration, Sister Thea Bowman combined the African American experience and religious sensibility with the rich spirituality of St. Francis and St. Clare. The result was the gift of herself to the Catholic Church, Black America, and the nation. To white Catholics she brought Black faith and a call to end racism. Among African Americans she opened hearts to the Catholic faith and the practical teachings of St. Francis. She taught in white schools, Black schools, and on college campuses. In every space she entered, Sister Thea Bowman was her full self, fully woman, fully Black, and fully Catholic.

As an African American woman from the South, immersed in Franciscan spirituality, her experience created a unique theology. Her interactions led to a conviction that God's love as lived through the universal Church could lead to the unity our world desperately needs. Bowman believed that, as members of the Body of Christ, we have a spiritual obligation to share our lives with others. She was one of the few Catholic leaders comfortable talking about Black liberation at historically Black Howard University as they were presenting Franciscan spirituality to a predominantly white audience.

Decades before Black Lives Matter, Sister Thea Bowman was a bold witness for racial justice. Her lectures and presentations among Black, Catholic, and general audiences were unforgettable. A superior of a Benedictine Order recounted how hearing Sister Thea decades earlier still resounded in her heart. Another person remarked that when he first heard Sister Thea, he knew he was in the presence of a saint. Catholics of all races have had their journeys enriched through encounters with the words and deeds of Sister Thea Bowman. Her influence in Black America can be measured by Harry Belafonte's interest in producing a feature film on her life.[7] Though it did not materialize, it reveals her impact on the Black freedom struggle, as Belafonte was an outspoken activist and supporter of movements for human dignity.

In 1984 Sister Thea was diagnosed with breast cancer. Though the illness and treatment impacted her ministry, she did not stop. Her witness was on full display at the 1989 U.S. Congress of Catholic Bishops meeting with her presentation, "What Does It Mean to Be Black and Catholic?"[8] Even with her strength and mobility sapped by cancer and the ensuing treatments, she held the bishops spellbound. In answering her own question, she broke out in the slave spiritual, "Sometimes I Feel Like a Motherless Child," comparing life as a Black person in the Catholic Church to being motherless, a long way from home. She then continued,

> What does it mean to be black and Catholic? It means that I come to my church fully functioning. That doesn't frighten you, does it? I bring myself, my black self, all that I am, all that I have, all that I hope to become, I bring my whole history, my traditions, my experiences, my culture, my African American song and dance and gesture and movement and teaching and preaching and healing and responsibility as gifts to the Church.[9]

At the end of the session, standing up from her wheelchair with help from those next to her, Sister Thea asked the assembled bishops to stand, hold hands, and sing, "We Shall Overcome." This perhaps was the first time in history that America's bishops held hands and sang together.[10]

Despite her illness and terminal diagnosis, Thea Bowman remained a whirlwind of Black Catholic energy to the end. She spoke at a Eucharistic Congress in Kenya, cofounded the National Black Sisters Conference, influenced the Institute of Black Catholic Studies at Xavier University, and spoke at several colleges and universities on Black Catholic pride.

In 1987 she was interviewed on *60 Minutes*, the groundbreaking news show of the era. Host Mike Wallace, upon first learning that he was going to interview a Black nun, was not impressed. Yet, following the interview, he wrote,

> I don't remember when I have been more moved, more enchanted, by a person whom I have profiled, than by Sister Thea Bowman. I confess I was a little skeptical when she was first suggested to me, but just one session with this remarkable individual convinced me; her openness, her compassion, her intelligence, her optimism, her humor captured me.[11]

Sixty million people in five nations watched that episode, and the news station and Sister Thea were flooded with positive comments in the weeks to come.

After her death on March 30, 1990, Thea Bowman's spirit lives on. Whenever we sing from the hymnal *Lead Me, Guide Me* (an African American Catholic hymnal), whenever Black Catholics gather at the Institute of Black Catholic Studies, whenever Franciscan peacemaking meets the Black justice tradition, we are living the legacy of Sister Thea Bowman.

> Sometimes people think they have to do big things in order to make change, but if each one of us would light a candle we'd have a tremendous light.[12]

3. SISTER SIMONE CAMPBELL, SSS

IN THE 1950S, SIMONE CAMPBELL and her sister Katy were raised Catholic in the fast-growing city of Long Beach south of Los Angeles. In those postwar years, America was ascendant as capitalism churned out increasing material benefits for many Americans. She was a young white girl with a bright future of material security and contentment. This trajectory, however, was changed by three events in her life.

The first came with her preteen reception of first communion. The Eucharist, for young Simone, was more than just another task on the confirmation "to-do list." Campbell later wrote in her book, *A Nun on the Bus*:

> There was this explosion for me, at the time I didn't fully understand it. I just knew I felt different. It was as if I was just being freed of something. That feeling, that sense, that definition of the eucharist, has never really left me, and I consider it one of the great graces of my life. And at the same time, it wasn't just a spiritual feeling; the experience led me deeper into the Catholic Church as a community.[13]

The next transformative event was the diagnosis of her beloved sister Katy with lymphoma. Katy's diagnosis was terminal, and Simone soon realized her lifelong friend would not be with her long. Seeing her vibrant sister slowly fade away and eventually die motivated her to live not just for herself but also for Katy.

The third event was television coverage of the 1963 Birmingham marches where Black children were assaulted by attack dogs and high-pressure fire hoses. The scenes of children marching peacefully then holding onto each other or braced against walls to keep from being tossed about were seared in her memory. Such sanctioned violence against the innocent repelled Simone and her dying sister Katy. Both Katy and Simone vowed then to work for racial justice. Knowing Katy would not live much longer, Simone intensified her commitment. She later wrote, "It just seeped into my bones, this sense that I needed to live intensely enough for both of us, to channel her passion as well as mine. As she grew weaker, my commitment only grew stronger."[14]

Those three experiences led Simone to consider a life devoted to God and humanity as a sister. Thus, she entered the Catholic religious community of the Sisters of Social Service. The community was founded by Sister Margaret Schlachta in Hungary in 1925, with a focus on service and a particular devotion to the Holy Spirit. Sister Margaret wrote that the Sisters of Social Service were to be placed in "exposed fields and sent onto unbroken roads…many times there will be no written guidance, every problem being different; therefore there will be no trenches in which to hide. The sisters must think very much, still more understand and mostly sense (the way forward)."[15]

Four years after joining the community, Sister Simone lost her sister Katy, and she noted, "That's where my sorrow went. Into the work. What I realized was that, in a way, I had picked up my sister's energy."[16]

One of her first "unbroken road" assignments was as a tenant rights organizer in Portland, Oregon, working with low-income and impoverished families. Simone then went to Los Angeles to work with at-risk adults. Her challenges in Portland and Los Angeles demonstrated to her that she could serve the poor more effectively as a lawyer. She went to law school, and shortly after finishing, she founded the Community Law Center to advocate for those who could not afford legal services.

After years of helping the poor and marginalized through her legal work, she was appointed director of Jericho, a lobby with the California State Legislature for policies on behalf of the poor. Here Sister Simone's efforts would have statewide and structural impacts. Her influence expanded to the national scene when she became executive director of NETWORK in 2004. NETWORK is the national lobbying arm of religious orders in the United States in areas of health care, racial justice, economic opportunity, and other causes. Forty-seven sisters from several religious orders founded NETWORK in 1972 when they realized national policies and federal intervention were critical to enhancing human dignity. Catholic social teaching regarding the dignity of the human person and social justice had to become a voice on Capitol Hill.

The sisters who worked in cities, suburbs, and rural areas knew the terrible costs of little to no health coverage on poor families and children. They witnessed unnecessary sicknesses and early deaths among the families they served. Therefore, when President Barack Obama sought to expand health care for more Americans, the sisters of NETWORK were a persistent presence in the House and Senate to urge support for the bill. After months of debate and discussion, on March 21, 2010, the House adopted the Patient Protection and Affordable Care Act (ACA) to bring health insurance to millions. Obama later credited NETWORK as the "tipping point" in the bill's passage.[17] Sister Simone Campbell's work with NETWORK opened national spaces for her Catholic commitment to justice. In 2012 she spoke at the Democratic

National Convention, and eight years later offered prayers at that same event.

Many Catholic bishops perceived the passage of the Affordable Care Act as enabling abortion rights. In 2009 the Vatican had begun a doctrinal assessment of the Leadership Conference of Religious Women (LCRW) on assertions that the sisters did not follow traditional Catholic teaching. After passage of the ACA, NETWORK, without notice, was included in this investigation. Both the LCRW and NETWORK were accused of focusing on feminist and social justice issues while neglecting orthodox teachings on gay marriage and abortion. The investigation also accused Sister Simone Campbell, NETWORK, and the Leadership Conference of being "radical feminists."[18]

Sister Simone and the sisters were not silent. Sister Simone later said that the bishops' support of the investigation was in part due to pressure from the pedophilia crisis and the need to focus attention elsewhere.[19] She also believed that "the bishops were upset because we won on health care. It's the old 'create a villain and attack,' but they picked the wrong target."[20] Sister Simone and the LCRW responded to the investigation of their work with "Nuns on the Bus," a national bus tour garnering support both for the organization and the Affordable Care Act. In addition, Sister Simone spoke to the nation on *60 Minutes*, was interviewed by *Rolling Stone* magazine, and was heard in many other venues.

Anchored in the Eucharist, inspired by her sister Katy, and imprinted with a commitment to justice through scenes of marching Black children, Simone Campbell lived a life of service for the outcast. When she retired from NETWORK in 2021, her legacy of service continued to live on in the policies, institutions, and individuals she helped transform.

Sister Simone Campbell, SSS

The spiritual life has led me to surprising spaces that are both sacred and awe-filled—and at times not a little frightening. At each twist and turn I have been keenly aware—or soon became aware, of the presence of the divine. It has been my long-standing spiritual practice to reflect daily and to try and become aware of what I am being called to do....It isn't easy, but at the heart of the lived experience, as in all of life, that call, and our response, is a sacred gift.[21]

4. SISTER ANITA CASPARY, IHM

IN 1970, OVER THREE HUNDRED Sisters of the Immaculate Heart of Mary (IHM) surrendered their vows and status in the Roman Catholic Church and became a lay ecumenical community. Sister Anita Caspary's *Witness to Integrity: The Crisis in the Immaculate Heart Community of California* describes the background and impacts of this remarkable story of dissent and courage. To voluntarily separate from the Roman Catholic Church, after taking vows of poverty, chastity, and obedience, does not come easily.

The seeds of their convictions were planted by the two prior mothers general of the order, Mother Eucharia (Elizabeth) Harney (served 1939–51) and Mother Regina (Josephine) McPartlin (served 1951–63). Both stimulated intellectual dialogue and authentic service to others. They often invited guest speakers whose perspectives sometimes challenged those of the Catholic hierarchy. Caspary wrote of Mother Eucharia, "She brought to all with whom she came in contact a reminder of the essential spirit of Christian love...rather than the letter of the law."[22] Consequently, the community's charism upheld the dignity of each human person and judged institutions, rules, laws, and leaders by the extent to which they affirmed human dignity and one's common humanity.

The spirit established by Mothers Eucharia and Regina was confirmed and elevated by the teachings of Vatican II. The Immaculate Heart of Mary community ran an influential high school and college in Los Angeles. The order promoted students' religious expressions through art and poetry, advocated for human rights and solidarity with those on the margins, and worked to live out the principles of Vatican II and the Catholic social teachings. Through their schools and other services, IHM sisters influenced lives throughout Los Angeles and beyond.

The Diocese of Los Angeles was headed by Cardinal James Francis McIntyre, an outspoken opponent of some of the changes inaugurated by Vatican II. His dislike for Vatican II took concrete form in his treatment of the IHM nuns. Sister Anita Caspary recounts being called to a meeting with Cardinal McIntyre. During the meeting, he peppered her with questions about the speakers they invited to campus, their use of modern art, and the books and materials used in their schools. From his perspective, the IHM sisters were acting contrary to proper Catholic doctrine and teaching. Unsatisfied with Sister Anita's answers and her refusal to admit wrong, the cardinal stormed out of the meeting shouting, "You will suffer for this."[23]

One of the many "transgressions" of the IHM order was its inclusion of non-Catholic writers in courses offered in the high school and college. They took seriously Vatican II's document, *Gaudium et Spes,* the Church in the Modern World, which proclaimed, "The joys and hopes...of the people of our time..., are the joys and hopes of the followers of Jesus Christ" (1). In addition, their spiritual formation was influenced by writings and lectures from Bernard Häring, Karl Rahner, Daniel Berrigan, Hans Küng, Robert McAfee Brown, Martin Marty, Cardinal Leon-Joseph Suenens, and others who lived Vatican II's call for a pilgrim church in service to the world.

The cardinal's outburst prompted a diocesan "visitation." The visitation included priests asking humiliating questions about the prayers, Mass attendance, political perspectives, theology readings, and sexual perspectives of the IHM sisters.

Following the visitation and the resulting dictates and demands, the IHM sisters, led by Sister Anita Caspary, held tear-filled times of prayer and reflection to determine their next steps. Among the potential outcomes of the visitation were removal of their teaching stipends, closure of the school and college, and even excommunication.

The IHM sisters, as devoted Catholics, attempted to respond with humility and grace to the demands for "reform" by the cardinal. They sought counsel from theologians and church officials such as Superior General Father Pedro Arrupe, SJ, and German moral theologian Bernard Häring. The IHM sisters proposed several changes for their order, which Cardinal McIntrye dismissed as inadequate. The IHM community was then subjected to further "visitations" and more demands.

Cardinal McIntrye and the Vatican were requiring absolute submission of the order to a demeaning array of demands and requirements. Among the draconian penalties imposed by the cardinal was exclusion from teaching in the diocese and a detailed series of penitential acts to be approved by priests and the bishop. Rather than submit to these demands, the IHM sisters chose to follow their understanding of God's call rather than the orders from a male-dominated hierarchy. There was a complex array of legal, property, and ecclesiastical issues to be resolved, and in the end, over three hundred IHM sisters refused to submit to the cardinal's will and resigned.[24]

Before and after resigning, the IHM sisters spent months in prayer, discussion, and consultation with others. While out of step with the hierarchy, they were still in vibrant union with Christ. Their discernment resulted in the formation of an independent ecumenical community called the Immaculate Heart Community. This decision reverberated throughout the Catholic world in general and the Los Angeles community in particular. Each IHM sister signed a commitment statement as they left the IHM order and formed the Immaculate Heart Community. Hundreds of sisters of the IHM, formerly an integral part of the Diocese of Los Angeles and the institutional church, became an independent ecumenical community serving God in the world. The creation of the community was not a step away from their spiritual commitments and devotion to God and service. In fact, when Father Bernard Häring read the founding decrees of the community, he said to Anita Caspary, "These Decrees require women of extraordinary strength, do you have such women?"[25]

The Immaculate Heart Community opened membership to married women and men, non-Catholics, and anyone committed to the principles of Christian service in the world. The work of the Immaculate Heart Community continued with ministries in family empowerment, an art center, and a retreat center. In addition, the Immaculate Heart School continued, with a remarkable rate of college-bound graduates.

The creation of the IH Community reminds us that our commitment to God's reign on earth and our understanding of what it means to follow Christ cannot always be aligned with the institution and structure of the church. As John of the Cross reminds us in *The Spiritual Canticle*, 37:4, if you consider all that God has revealed to saints and prophets over the centuries, the greater part is yet to be understood.[26] God is indeed beyond our institutions, creeds, traditions, and leaders. Caspary captures the vision in the following statement:

> Our renewal, which was ultimately a revolution, was accomplished only by an insistence on trusting our collective participation, which led us to a

communal and practical vision. We believed that the Spirit of God was with us....What we have lost in canonical recognition we gained in public witness to resist an authoritative and abusive Church system of control. We gained joy and peace and freedom to worship, serve and love. As a Christian ecumenical community, our rituals...are not confined by male-privileged rules and prohibitions. We are free to serve in the public and private realms of life. As attorneys, educators, professors, nurses, mothers and fathers, social workers, foster-mothers, scholars, musicians, secretaries, retreat and shelter directors, we continue to expand our understanding of being a Christian in the world. We are free to love and form committed relationships that enhance our service to the world.[27]

5. SISTER MARY ANTONA EBO, FSM

SEVERAL IMAGES OF THE CIVIL rights movement endure. Photographs captured the spirit, courage, and essence of a struggle that, still unfinished, transformed the nation and expanded rights for African Americans. These images moved hearts and gave greater depth to the meaning of "liberty and justice for all." Among these iconic images are Emmett Till's open casket, children hurled aside by fire hoses, Rosa Parks gazing out the window from her bus seat, the Rev. Dr. Martin Luther King Jr. in front of the Lincoln Memorial, and Fannie Lou Hamer speaking over the microphone at the 1964 Democratic Convention. Among these memorable photographs is one of Sister Mary Antona Ebo, a Black nun, leading a delegation of five white nuns and some clergy members at the 1965 Selma to Montgomery March for Voting Rights.

Sister Mary Antona Ebo of the Sisters of St. Mary (SSM)—later renamed Franciscan Sisters of Mary (FSM)—in the habit of her religious order at the front of a march demanding racial justice and political equality had vast implications. First, it demonstrated to African Americans that the Catholic Church, or at least a small sector of it, stood in solidarity with their issues. Prior to her stand, most African Americans assumed, rightly, that the white Catholic Church supported the status quo of inequality and white supremacy. Sister Mary Antona Ebo was a visible counter to that image. Second, her stand shook thousands of white Catholics from indifference to activism. Sister Mary Peter Traxler, as head of the National Catholic Conference for Interracial Justice wrote, "Like the faithful women of the Gospel, Sisters must follow Christ into the world ministering to His needs in the person of the poor, the sick, the persecuted."[28] Traxler added, "After Selma, you can't stay home again."[29]

On the day of the march, Sister Mary Antona spoke to the crowd gathered at the Brown African Methodist Episcopal Church, "I am here today because I am a Negro, a nun, a Catholic, and because I want to bear witness."[30] Author Shannen Dee Williams details her story in her brilliant work, *Subversive Habits: Black Catholic Nuns in the Long African American Freedom Struggle*. Williams records that many in the crowd had never seen a Black nun, and certainly not one at a protest. Those who knew African American nuns existed likely assumed they would be found in cloisters instead of the streets. The image of a protesting Black nun was so unnerving that many whites in Selma assumed a Black woman was posing in costume.

The march that attracted Sister Mary Antona occurred three days after Bloody Sunday, where mounted police officers had charged, bludgeoned, and assaulted unarmed marchers. Earlier in Selma, a group of white men had murdered white Unitarian minister James Reeb, and Alabama was historically home to hundreds of lynchings, beatings, threats, intimidations, firings, and other assaults on Black people. Sister Mary Antona's presence both as a participant and a leader of a delegation was a public and risky move. In Alabama, a Black woman would not be shielded from violence because of her habit or profession of faith.

Flying in from St. Louis, she declared, "I don't want to be a martyr, but it was either put up or shut up."[31] The impact of her presence was evident as soon as she stepped off the plane in Selma. Edmundite father Maurice Ouellet, SSE, white pastor of the city's only African American Catholic parish, was there to welcome her and the others. When the habit-wearing dark-skinned Sister Mary Antona Ebo got off the plane, he later said, "She was as black as black could be. And I said to myself, oh God this is going to make a difference."[32] Ouellet had been secretly supporting civil rights and understood the cost of commitment. Sister Mary Antona Ebo merged color and Catholicism into a symbol of justice. When she said she wanted to "bear witness," Sister Mary Antona referred to the witness of a Black woman standing with her people, and a religious sister standing on behalf of the reign of God on earth.

Selma was not her first, only, or last witness. When she was eighteen, Elizabeth Louise Ebo (later Mary Antona) desegregated Holy Trinity High School in Bloomington, Illinois. Feeling a call to serve humanity in general and her race in particular, she attempted to enroll in a Catholic nursing school, but the white sisters denied her application. Undeterred, she moved to St. Louis and enrolled in St. Mary's Infirmary School, at the time the only Black Catholic nursing school in the nation. Determined to serve God through a consecrated life, she was among the first three African American women admitted to the Sisters of St. Mary.[33]

Shannen Dee Williams recounts the "uncommon faithfulness" of Sister Mary Antona Ebo. Despite the admission of Black sisters, the Sisters of St. Mary practiced racial discrimination and marginalization at every turn. The Black sisters' profession of vows was a segregated event, as were dining arrangements, assignments, and other activities. Sister Mary Antona's belief that the Gospel called us to full life, and that Jesus was Savior, Friend, and Liberator, kept her faithful to the order. She resisted these daily affronts to her dignity, growing more outspoken with each encounter.

Her boldness displayed in Selma is but a snapshot into her life of faith and struggle. When she believed race was a factor in her denied request to be active in the National Catholic Conference for Interracial Justice, she protested.

Sister Mary Antona wrote to the conference leadership that their outright denial of her application was evidence that whiteness was a more important quality than an applicant's God-given gifts and obvious calling. She asserted that God called Black women to service, and that calling should not be stifled by superiors who looked more to race than to the Holy Spirit.

In 1968, Sister Mary Antona Ebo was one of the founders of the National Black Catholic Sisters Conference (NBCSC). This organization was the response of Black nuns to the racist violence that claimed the lives of Dr. Martin Luther King Jr., Medgar Evers, and many others. The NBCSC gave Black nuns a place of healing, encouragement, and inspiration to continue their struggle for justice. Sister Mary Antona was a featured speaker at the first conference and reminded those gathered of their unique gifts of Black Catholicism. Decades later, she served as president of the NBCSC, and in 1989 the conference awarded her the Harriet Tubman Award for being "called to be a Moses to the people."[34]

Sister Mary Antona Ebo bore witness in Selma, in her religious order, at the NBCSC, and in every place she entered. She had master's degrees in hospital executive development and theology of health care and was a certified chaplain through the National Association of Catholic Chaplains. In hospitals, schools, and clinics, Sister Mary Antona lived her vocation in service to humanity.

Her voice was heard on behalf of justice long after Selma. In a 2011 interview with the Catholic News Service, she said she hoped the memorial to Dr. King would prompt "soul-searching" by the nation. Such soul-searching, she hoped, would usher in a new day of justice and equality. She also noted, "If we have to keep talking about keeping the dream alive, then what have we been doing for it still to be a dream? Martin was our dreamer. His dream was for his time. Who are our dreamers today?"[35] In 2014, ninety-year-old Sister Mary Antona Ebo went to Ferguson, Missouri, following the murder of Michael Brown. She told reporters on the scene, "You are not here to take a superficial picture....You are going to raise up the rug and look at what's under the rug."[36] For Ebo, Brown's killing was another thread in the fabric of American injustice. From St. Louis to Selma to the NBCSC to Ferguson, Sister Mary Antona Ebo brought Catholic devotion from the prayer chapel to the streets.

6. SISTER M. MARTIN DE PORRES GREY, RSM / PATRICIA GREY, PHD

AS A YOUNG BLACK CATHOLIC WOMAN, Patricia Grey became the first African American woman to join the Religious Sisters of Mercy in Pittsburgh. She found that white supremacy, racism, and racial ignorance infected religious orders as much as or more than the society at large. Grey, like other Black sisters, faced obstacles far beyond the discipline required for a life of prayer, contemplation, and works of mercy. Grey held on to her roots, for once she became a formal member of the order, she took the name of the Black saint of Peru and was known as Sister M. Martin de Porres Grey.

A turning point in the United States and in the life of Patricia Grey was the year 1968 in which the seeds of the National Black Catholic Clergy Caucus were planted at a gathering in Pittsburgh. Along with the male priests and seminarians, however, was the unexpected and unsettling presence of twenty-five-year-old Sister M. Martin de Porres Grey. She was not the only initial attendee who was not a Black priest, as white activist priest Father Dan Mallette and Black laymen Joseph Davis also came to the first meeting.[37] The sixty Black priests were anxious to build a community of support, and in the early stages they had several discussions on whether white priests, Black women religious, or Black laypersons should be allowed to join. After a vigorous and sometimes heated debate, Davis was allowed to remain as an observer, while Grey and Mallette were excluded.[38]

Father Mallette left, but Sister M. Martin de Porres remained, refusing to leave on the grounds that Black solidarity was more important than male collegiality, and that the work for justice must override both race and gender. Standing alone against unaccepting Black priests, Grey argued her presence was a matter of justice and solidarity. Her powerful arguments swayed the position of some of the Black priests, and she was allowed to remain as an unofficial observer. This limited role allowed her to stay without voice, vote, or even status as an attendee in the minutes.

Author Shannen Dee Williams records that though Grey was disappointed in her limited status, she was moved by the emotional descriptions of racism experienced by the Black priests. Before leaving, she appealed again that Black religious sisters be part of the caucus. She later said:

> I got up and suggested they open the caucus to sisters and allow us to participate fully. I pointed out there are too few Catholic priests....For this reason the black priests ought to combine forces with us... and our power will begin to be heard....Well, it caused quite a stir....I challenged them openly on the matter and accused them of prejudice against their own women.[39]

Imagine one young woman, speaking truth to sixty men, all of whom were older or held the status of ordination. The majority of priests ignored her petition, but her work was just beginning. Energized by the vision of united Black Catholics, Grey departed and sought to organize a national Black sisters gathering. Father James Patterson Lyke, OFM, who later coordinated the publication of the African American hymnal *Lead Me, Guide Me* and became the second Black archbishop in the United States, further encouraged her efforts to bring Black sisters together for mutual support.

Sister M. Martin de Porres contacted by letter every mother superior in the nation and many around the world, particularly in Africa and the Caribbean. Her letter astutely noted that a Black sisters' gathering would give them the strength and fortitude to remain loyal members of their respective congregations. She also argued that support from congregations of religious sisters would counter the impression among African Americans that the Catholic Church cared little about Black life. Despite the brilliance of her arguments, most mother superiors either never responded to her letter, opposed the concept, or had no Black sisters within their congregations. From the 633 letters she sent, she received two hundred responses.[40] Most of those responses opposed the concept, arguing that an all-Black gathering was counter to the unity of the Gospel. Such a view was ironic given that they themselves often participated in all-white gatherings with no sense of exclusivity. Grey also faced opposition from many bishops and priests, concerned about both an all-Black meeting and a meeting of women without oversight from the hierarchy.

Despite racism, intransigence, and patriarchy, Sister M. Martin de Porres delivered a modern miracle. On August 17, 1968, 155 Black sisters from the United States, the Caribbean, and Africa gathered in Pittsburgh at Mount Mercy College for the first ever Black Sisters Conference.

It is perhaps impossible to capture the energy, pride, and spirit present when over one hundred Black women with a devoted religious commitment converged for the first time with others like themselves. Their coming together was for many a freeing release from years of insults and indifference in their white orders. Also, for most, this was their first encounter with other Black sisters. While many had subordinated their Black culture and imagination in the suffocating confines of religious life, others had kept that flame alive. Black sisters in Black religious orders were energized to see they had colleagues struggling in white orders. No matter their prior level of activism, most if not all the participants returned home with a renewed sense of their unique and vital role as Black women religious.

During the administrative portion of the meeting, the sisters created a national organization, the National Black Sisters Conference (NBSC), with an executive board and an agenda for future work. Father Charles Burns, SVD, who had attended the Black Clergy Conference and had supported Grey becoming a full voting member, attended the Black Sisters Conference out of solidarity. He noted, "There was more love there, there was far more intensity of purpose…so much beautiful work."[41]

The next year at the University of Dayton, speakers energized the Black nuns with insights from nonviolent protest, gospel music, Black theology, and Pan-African history. Shannen Williams notes, "They sought to become visible in secular Black society in new and important ways, triggering a new dimension in Black women's political activism."[42] In addition to their roles in nursing, teaching, and mentoring, many NBSC sisters became activists against police brutality, discrimination, and inequality. They were assertive and often well-connected, for the NBSC sisters were some of the most educated Black women in the country. In many cases, they were already civil rights leaders in their respective arenas, even before the NBSC. Since the Catholic Church was often as segregated as secular society, many of these women faced and overcame rigid racial barriers in their religious orders, convents, schools, and colleges long before *Brown v. Board of Education* and new civil rights laws.

The National Black Sisters Conference continues to gather, empower, and act for justice. Although Sister M. Martin de

Porres Grey left her order in 1973, her legacy continues. Black sisters, even with aging members and declining numbers, continue the work and message of the 1968 Black Sisters Conference. When the leader of the U.S. Conference of Catholic Bishops criticized Black Lives Matter, the NBSC responded with a letter outlining the theological and moral flaws with that position.[43] The influence of Sister M. Martin de Porres and the NBSC lives on in the work of Black sisters and in the people they have served.

> We black religious women see ourselves as gifted with the choicest of God's blessings. The gift of our womanhood, that channel through which the Son of God Himself chose to come into the human race, endows us with those qualities...which are designed for the deliverance of humanity....And the gift of our religious vocation makes accessible to us that union with Christ which guides us to the task, strengthens our determination and sustains our efforts to free ourselves and our black brethren from the intolerable burden forced upon us as victims of racism.[44]

7. SISTER THERESA HARPIN, CSJ

"I THOUGHT I WAS NOTHING, but now I'm something." This testimony graces the website of Restorative Partners, San Luis Obispo, California.[45] Restorative Partners is a nonprofit organization serving current and formerly incarcerated people on the central coast of California. Similar to other restorative justice programs across the nation, Restorative Partners works to create new outlooks and perspectives among those they serve. They do not define people by the crimes for which they were incarcerated but as humans seeking redemption. Restorative Partners addresses accountability, focuses on spiritual formation, provides mentoring programs, identifies employment, and offers clean and sober living space. This work transforms lives.

Restorative Partners believes that each person always is "something," despite family circumstances, social pressures, economic forces, and personal failures that shouted, "You are nothing." Restorative Partners returns the "somethingness" to people whose behaviors and crimes lead to arrest, conviction, and prison.

Restorative Partners began in the heart and mind of Sister Theresa Harpin of the Sisters of St. Joseph of Carondelet. In describing her journey from childhood to founder of Restorative Partners, Sister Theresa incorporates the totem pole image from Indigenous peoples, highlighting the transformative moments of her life.[46]

The first was a series of encounters with her great-aunt, Sister George Arthur of the Sisters of Providence. Her great-aunt lived for a while with young Teresa's grandparents;

during this time, Teresa closely observed her lifestyle and was impressed by her humility and prayerfulness. Sister Theresa noted, "She meant something deeply in my life, her relationship with Christ stood out and was obvious, and was manifest in her by being loving, kind and good."

Next on the totem pole was her teacher in third grade, Sister Isabel Espinoza, OP. Sister Isabel "instilled in me a thirst for God, for that is what I saw in her." Her teacher was instrumental in Theresa's first communion, and during that Mass "it was there I fell in love with the idea that I could commune with God." Even as a child, from the influence of her great-aunt and her third-grade teacher, Theresa grasped that the encounter with Christ in the Eucharist is personal, transformational, and filled with grace that overflows into our daily lives. She also adds that "what I learned from her was that faith is not for ourselves but is for the life of the world."

Theresa also recalls the simple ways Sister Isabel taught the value of service. There were a few left-handed students in the class with Theresa, and Sister Isabel was unable to teach handwriting to them as a right-handed person. Sister Isabel asked Theresa to help her teach the left-handed students how to write. Through this small act, Theresa gained a profound sense of service and the value of helping others.

Sister Isabel saw how much Theresa enjoyed helping others, so she also asked her to help clean the convent chapel. This work gave Theresa a sense of pride and the feeling that she helped enhance the religious community's worship experience. Sister Isabel also loved St. Therese of Lisieux. She often quoted from her autobiography, *Story of a Soul*, and tried to imitate the life of "The Little Flower." Theresa Harpin was named after Therese of Lisieux, and so Sister Isabel enjoyed teaching Theresa the virtues, prayers, and life of her namesake. She gave her books and holy cards about

St. Therese, and later added a gift that Theresa Harpin has kept for decades. Sister Isabel ordered a first-class relic of the French saint, all the way from Rome, and gave this treasure to her student Theresa. The relic remains a prized possession of Theresa Harpin, a reminder of the generosity of Sister Isabel and the life and legacy of the saint who said, "Your love has preceded me, become greater in my youth, and is now an abyss whose depth I cannot fathom."[47]

Theresa Harpin later attended the Academy of Our Lady of Peace in San Diego, California, another totem moment. The school was run by the Sisters of St. Joseph of Carondelet. By this time, the previous encounters had shaped and developed a growing faith in Theresa. That faith was further refined by the sisters at the academy. She remembers, "The sisters there had so much joy, always laughing, teaching, and helping others. They were always welcoming, inclusive and empowering." When her father lost his business, the Harpin family could no longer afford the tuition. The sisters found Theresa a job on campus, and she was able to pay her tuition and remain in school.

All these encounters with religious sisters led Theresa Harpin to pursue a consecrated life as a Sister of St. Joseph of Carondelet. She took her religious vows in 1971. Sister Theresa Harpin sought to live the life she had seen in her great-aunt, Sister Isabel, and the Sisters at Our Lady of Peace. Over the years she served as a pastor, a campus minister, a musician, and a parish social justice coordinator.

In 2005 she visited Sister Suzanne Jabro, CSJ, a sister from her order who began a program connecting children with their incarcerated mothers. This program, called Get on the Bus, was inspired during a visit to a women's prison in California when Sister Suzanne asked the incarcerated mothers the last time they had seen their children. Most answered, "It's been years," primarily due to finances, lack of transportation, and the distant rural location of most prisons. That inspired Sister Suzanne and others to begin Get on the Bus, where bus trips are arranged to allow for half-day visits in the women's prison. Sister Theresa Harpin was familiar with the California Men's Colony in San Luis Obispo and offered to do a similar program there. What began as a bus originating in Los Angeles to San Luis Obispo expanded to eighteen buses from all over California. Testimony and studies both agree that family contact with incarcerated parents increases the likelihood of inmates' success upon release and helps the children overcome the stigma of "your mother/father is in jail."

The success of Get on the Bus and the relationships she established with fathers in prison inspired Sister Theresa to create Restorative Partners. She had become increasingly aware of the challenges the formerly incarcerated face upon release. Internal attitudes and external prejudices create almost insurmountable obstacles for a man or woman released after years in prison. Restorative Partners, founded in 2011, works to complement spiritual and mental transformation with opportunities for work and housing.

Restorative Partners began with seeds planted by religious sisters in various schools and communities decades earlier. Sister Theresa later said, "The most important thing is that these women taught me how to pray. And that the most important thing you can have in life is to have a relationship with God."

When asked how she was able to expand Get on the Bus and create Restorative Partners, she answered, "Faith and action are the same thing, the action is what happens on the outside, but flows from what happens on the inside, from what God puts on my heart." The Restorative Partners website summarizes their underlying convictions:

Sister Theresa Harpin, CSJ

We believe in accompanying and supporting anyone affected by crime on their healing journey, to be an instrument of restoration, of forgiveness, of accountability, and of reconciliation. We believe violence is never a solution to any problem and that every person is endowed with a sacred dignity, and is capable of changing, healing and being restored.[48]

8. SISTER LAURA VICUÑA PEREIRA MANSO, CF

AS A YOUNG GIRL GROWING UP IN the Amazon rainforest, Laura Vicuña Pereira Manso learned of two realities. One was that Brazil's Indigenous people were considered obstacles to progress and the accumulation of wealth and natural resources. Her other reality was that religious faith, specifically Catholicism, urged believers to embrace the pain and agony of their fellow human beings. Her family were migrants from northeast Brazil, members of the Indigenous Kariri people of that region. She recalls that her family never spoke of their past. Laura Manso later found that centuries of exploitation, massacres, and repression by the government, the military, and corporate economic forces on their own ancient lands had systematically erased their customs, traditions, religion, art, and often their language.

These two realities, or in the words of Vatican II the "signs of the times," were the foundation of her life's calling. Laura's mother was a community leader and was involved with the Franciscan Catechist Sisters of that region. Influenced both by her mother and the Franciscan sisters, she later wrote, "I saw those nuns among the people, promoting actions to defend their lives, and that always attracted me, I wanted to be like them."[49] Her desire to emulate the dedication of the sisters led her to join the order when she was thirteen years old.

Sister Laura Vicuña Pereira Manso, CF, devoted her life to God, simplicity, and service to the poor. Her vocation fit that of the order, which was founded to serve the neediest in our world. She said of her vocation:

> I think that the church is an ally of great potential for the people, for the leaders in the community, who are part of this work. The church that I was born in, that I have learned from my mother, is this church that is with their people, that is in the midst of the people, who walk together with the people. It's this presence of the church that is next to them without doing many things. Just being a presence.[50]

This sentiment was underscored by another of her colleagues, Sister Lucia Gianesini, who noted, "Many don't know we are nuns. All they know is that it is really good when we visit them.[51] Sister Laura and her community are a "presence" whose visits among the exploited, poor, and Indigenous people bring good in the midst of difficulty.

As global corporations and agribusiness seek to extract the wealth of the Amazon, the Indigenous people who call those lands home are often forced from their traditional villages. In some cases, gunmen harass or even kill some of the land's original inhabitants and their advocates. Among the peoples that the Franciscan Catechist Sisters work with are the Uru Eu Wau Wau, the Kariri, and the Karipuna. Despite years of oppression, the Kariri people—Sister Laura's heritage—continue to exist.

The ancestral lands of the Indigenous people of Brazil's Amazon rainforest are under constant encroachment and invasion by forces of "progress" and "development." The worst years were from the 1960s through the 1980s when the military junta allowed a virtual war against the Indigenous people of that land. Even today, ranchers, loggers, and miners devastate the fragile lands and rainforest occupied by Indigenous peoples. Often forced to hide deep in the forest, Indigenous villagers have little protection. Standing in this breach are Sister Laura Manso, the Franciscan Catechist Sisters, and others. The sisters are also part of a larger organization, the Brazilian bishops' Indigenous Missionary Council (known by the Portuguese acronym CIMI), an organization that advocates for the territorial and human rights of Indigenous peoples in Brazil.

Sister Laura's particular gifts are empowering the women of the region and helping communities retain claim to their traditional lands. Manso and her colleagues follow the spirit of the Old Testament prophet Habakkuk, who proclaimed, "I will stand at my watchpost, and station myself on the rampart; I will keep watch to see what he will say to me" (Hab 2:1).

As a result of Sister Laura Manso's vocation, many Indigenous women have pursued educational paths that would have formerly been closed to them. They have obtained degrees in education, law, and other fields to help liberate their people from oppression. Sister Laura has also worked alongside the Indigenous peoples to protest incursions on their land, demand assistance from the government, and advocate for their rights to their lands.

Sister Laura Manso is an Indigenous sister confronting global economic forces, but she is not deterred. Public protests are risky, maneuvering the bureaucracy of government a test, and advocacy frustrating, but she persists. The archbishop of Porto Velho, Roque Paloschi, said she has helped restore Indigenous people's dignity, hope, and the possibility of dreaming. "She is active on different fronts, always advancing her vision of overcoming this patriarchal and misogynistic society."[52]

Sister Terezinha Dalcegio, CF, is the regional coordinator for Sister Laura's province. She said of her colleague, "She is always involved with the community's activities. I think church life is a kind of food for her soul."[53] The comparison of church life with the food for her soul reminds one of the power of the Eucharist. When Jesus says, "Do this, in memory of me," we envision "this" as the gift of his life. Sister Laura lives the Eucharist through her service, the food for her soul.

Pope Francis recognized Sister Laura's commitment in 2019 when he asked her to attend the Synod of Bishops for the Pan-Amazon Region. He later asked that she be a member of the recently established Ecclesial Conference of the Amazon Region.[54] Active in the Ecclesial Conference, Sister Laura Manso embodies the power of women in the ministry and life of the church. The Amazon is particularly challenging as few priests, remote locations, and long distances leave many parishes and communities without a priest. Into that gap steps women ministers like Sister Laura. As a result of her ministry and that of many other women, the Amazon Synod highlighted the critical role of women in the life of the church. There was also recognition that without women, the church in the Amazon would hardly exist. As she works among the Indigenous peoples, protests against unlawful incursions, or participates in the Ecclesial Conference of the Amazon Region, Sister Laura Manso reminds us that as church, we are to be present among, walk alongside, and bring "good news" to those most in need.

9. MARTYRED MISSIONARIES OF EL SALVADOR: JEAN DONOVAN, LAYPERSON; ITA FORD, MM; MAURA CLARKE, MM; AND DOROTHY KAZEL, OSU

POLITICS MATTER. WITH THE 1980 election of Ronald Reagan and the ensuing military conflict in El Salvador, oppression of the poor escalated, and it was open season on anyone remotely associated with human development instead of profits.

The civil war in El Salvador was hardly a battle of equals; on one side were peasants, Catholic base communities, activist religious and priests, and guerrillas. On the other side was the El Salvadoran military, backed by the most powerful nation on the planet, the United States.

Politics matter. Under the Democratic presidency of Jimmy Carter, attempts at human rights protection occurred. That wavering commitment evaporated with the election of Ronald Reagan. Jean Donovan, a lay missionary in El Salvador, felt a noticeable increase in military presence, violence, abductions, and oppression after Reagan's November election win. Given his campaign rhetoric, Reagan's election emboldened the El Salvadoran military.

This boldness was on brutal display on December 2, 1980. That day, lay missionary Jean Donovan and Ursuline sister Dorothy Kazel went to the airport in El Salvador to pick up Maryknoll sisters Ita Ford and Maura Clarke. On their return home, the four unarmed women were stopped by El Salvadoran soldiers and forced from their vehicle. The four were abducted, beaten, raped, and eventually killed. Villagers nearby heard pistol and machine gun shots, most likely the final violence inflicted on these messengers of hope and love. Their bodies were later found in a shallow grave.[55]

Without the silent complicity of the United States, no one in the El Salvadoran military would have allowed such a brutal and hideous attack on U.S. citizens. This was hinted at later when the parents of Jean Donovan contacted the State Department following her murder. They were upper-middle-class Republicans, and her father was chief of design for one of the Pentagon's largest military contractors, Sikorsky Aircraft. Since, however, their daughter's work alongside the poor made her a "communist," their credentials mattered little. Their first contacts were met with chilly responses. Later they were told to stop bothering State Department officials. There was more to come. President Ronald Reagan's administration later accused the women of "running a roadblock," "engaging in an exchange of gunfire," and of "not being nuns but political activists." As an ultimate insult, the Donovans received a bill for $3,500 for the cost of returning the brutalized body of their daughter back home.[56]

Just who were these roadblock-running, troublemaking activists who were kidnapped, beaten, raped, and murdered by allies of the United States government? Maryknoll sister Ita Ford was assigned to Chile in 1973, in the middle of the U.S.-supported coup that destroyed the administration of Salvador Allende. She ministered to the poor and displaced during a time of violent upheaval. Ford later responded to Archbishop Oscar Romero's request for people to come to El Salvador to support the innocents caught in the middle of a civil war that multiplied the misery of El Salvador's peasants.

Sister Ita moved to El Salvador to live among, empower, and bring Good News to the poor.[57]

Maryknoll sister Maura Clarke joined the order in 1953, noting a desire "to come closer to God and serve Him."[58] She served the poor in Nicaragua for many years, including a term from 1970 to 1976. Clarke was also in Managua following the massive 1972 earthquake, after which she helped the orphaned, displaced, and injured. She and other sisters helped form "base communities" wherein peasants were empowered to stand up for basic human dignities. She returned to the United States, served on the East Coast, and later experienced a spiritual renewal calling her back to Latin America. The horrific impacts of El Salvador's civil war were felt across the nation. Sister Maura Clarke and Sister Ita Ford together served the town of Chalatenango, El Salvador, where they helped families search for missing fathers and sons, bury the dead, pray with the families of prisoners, and work with the people to break the bonds of oppression, poverty, and violence.[59]

Ursuline sister Dorothy Kazel joined the order in 1960. She was a teacher and counselor for Indigenous people in Arizona. She taught the deaf and worked in interracial community programs. In 1974 she joined other Ursuline sisters in El Salvador, where she became known as "Madre Dorothea" as she visited the sick, helped mothers care for their children, and trained catechists to keep faith alive amid war and violence. Threats of kidnapping and death were never far from Sister Dorothy and her community. In facing her fears, she noted in her diary, "overcoming fear...to give my life for the service of others...to let the cross pierce my soul in the depths of my soul: to love the cross, to accept It totally."[60] By 1980, her ministry included burying the dead left behind by army troops and resettling refugees into centers. The scent of death was always near, as peasants and villagers would go missing under dubious circumstances.

The youngest of the four and the only layperson was Jean Donovan. She was twenty-six at the time of the brutal assault. After graduating in business administration, she was on the road to a prosperous career as a management consultant. In search of a richer meaning to her life, while volunteering for a youth ministry in Cleveland, she learned of the life of El Salvador's poor. In linking service to humanity with her Catholic faith, she told her friends, "I wanted to get closer to Him, and that's the only way I think I can."[61]

Donovan was also influenced by conversations with Father Michael Crowley, a priest who worked among Peru's poor. Seeking to hear where God was calling her, through prayer, contemplation, and conversation, Jean Donovan decided to serve El Salvador's poor as a lay servant. She arrived in El Salvador in 1979, a time of intensified violence against the poor and their supporters. She and Dorothy Kazel worked in La Libertad, where they clothed the destitute, fed the hungry, and cared for wounded refugees. The locals called her "St. Jean the Playful" in recognition of her joy and laughter despite the horrors of war. When her body was recovered from the shallow grave, it was noted that the face that once laughed was destroyed by the savage attackers.

Ita Ford, Maura Clarke, Dorothy Kazel, and Jean Donovan lost their lives in devotion to the Gospel of Christ and in service to our broken humanity. As horrible as their deaths were, they were but four of the seventy thousand people who perished in the U.S.-backed war against "leftists" and "troublemakers."

> Several times I have decided to leave El Salvador. I almost could except for the children, the poor bruised victims of this insanity. Who would care

for them? Whose heart would be so staunch as to favor the reasonable thing in a sea of their tears and helplessness? Not mine, dear friend, not mine.... I think that the hardship one endures maybe is God's way of taking you out into the desert and to prepare you to meet and love him more fully.[62]

Jean Donovan

I hope you come to find that which gives life a deep meaning for you. Something worth living for—maybe even worth dying for—something that energizes you, enthuses you, enables you to keep moving ahead. I can't tell you what it might be— that's for you to find, to choose, to love. I can just encourage you to start looking and support you in the search.[63]

Letter from Sister Ita Ford to her
sixteen-year-old godchild

10. SISTER EVELYN MONTEIRO, SCC

SISTER EVELYN MONTEIRO OF INDIA is among the many Asian Catholic women who find in their faith the inspiration, wisdom, and courage to proclaim the Gospel as good news for all those struggling for full humanity. Among those most in need of this message are the women of Asia. Patriarchy, misogyny, and male domination are so ingrained in many cultures that degradation and abuse of women is considered normal behavior. This oppression is amplified when justified by religious dogma and the edicts of a male god. The litany of realities facing women are restricted educational opportunities, domestic violence, rape, human trafficking, and the underlying status as property or sexual less-than-human objects.

In this climate, Indian nun Sister Evelyn Monteiro was moved by the words of Karl Rahner's *Theological Investigations*, vol. 8: *Further Theology of the Spiritual Life 2*, wherein he declares "a church of women themselves."[64] His words were not a new revelation; they merely confirmed what she already knew: women are essential for a vibrant Catholic Church. Her awareness rested on life as an Indian Catholic woman, from the faithfulness of Mary Magdalene, the love of Mary of Bethany, the service of Phoebe the Deacon (Rom 16:1), and the work of those in her order, the Sisters of the Holy Cross of Chavanod (SCC).

In 2001 Sister Evelyn gathered with other women from Asia to discuss ways they could advance the voice and presence of Asian Catholic women theologians and activists. These discussions led to a remarkable 2002 conference in Bangkok,

Thailand, where fifty-five Asian women gathered under the theme "The Voices of the Silenced."[65] This five-day event was historic in that it proclaimed, after millennia of male domination and life in a patriarchal institution, that women were emerging from the shadows. They affirmed that women were created in the image of God with talents and gifts necessary for the flourishing of the church and the world. By giving "voices" to those silenced through abuse of power, the very theme of the conference declared women's human dignity.

Sister Evelyn Monteiro gave the keynote address and referred to Rahner's reminder that theirs was a "church of women themselves," not women dependent upon men, not women subservient or secondary, but women leaders with voices and gifts, without whom there would be no church. Lectures, prayers, and liturgies urged Asian women theologians and religious leaders to elevate their spiritual powers and "redefine our collective struggle of doing theology, and reconstruct the distinctive nature of our emancipatory theological reflection."[66]

The name of the 2002 conference, the Theological Forum of Ecclesia of Women in Asia, was shortened to Ecclesia of Woman in Asia (EWA). Dr. Mary Yuen in a video titled "About EWA" spoke of Sister Evelyn's presentation and how the attendees were so energized that they determined this gathering would not be a "one-off" but an ongoing project.[67] Though their home nations and cultures were different, from Korea to Indonesia to India to Vietnam, they faced common struggles. The 2002 conference was not an abstract theological ramble. Confronted daily with the suffering of Asian women, these women did not allow their faith to devolve into pious proclamations or meaningless theological minutiae. Instead, God the Creator, Jesus the Liberator, and Sophia Holy Wisdom summoned them to urgent work for women's liberation. The closing liturgy, titled "The Liberator," was a compelling call to action. Several narrators shared these words:

> The women's shrieks and the agonizing wail of
> suffering humankind melts God's heart.
> She sends Her only Son to free us from the rule of
> sin.
> Words have become flesh and lived among us.
> To be remembered and celebrated in the form of
> unleavened bread and wine, Eucharist.
>
> After salvation,
> are we using the power of God's blessings to
> change our lives for the better?
>
> From all over the world, we hear the soft
> lamentation of Asia women who are oppressed
> and become the victims of violence.
>
> How can we commemorate and look at the
> Eucharistic bread and say: "This is My Body"
> While the bodies of women are tortured, raped,
> sterilized, chopped, enslaved, manipulated, and
> abused for the benefit of men?
>
> Once again, the Spirit of God does not stand still.
> She empowers the voices so that they are like
> ripples that disrupt the stability and comfort of
> the oppressors.
>
> The simultaneous ear-shattering wails and cries
> rock the Earth.
> Asian skies are bubbling in turbulence and the
> oceans are boiling in anger.
> Then, an honest vow and strong determination is

built among the children of God: Women and Men.

If we believe that at this moment,
God is still building freedom
through the sweat and tears of these men and women,
and that God is maintaining our freedom
through those who are still listening to their conscience.

We will see that liberation and freedom are not the end
Instead, a challenge for the Church community
An Ecclesia of Wo/men![68]

Embracing the Catholic use of physical objects as carriers of divine truth, participants used symbols throughout the closing liturgy. Candles symbolized enlightenment. A woman dressed in black carrying a bier represented violence and injustice toward women. The breaking of an earthen jar symbolized the end of silence. Flowers were symbols of compassion and empathy. The distribution of scarves to all in attendance represented loving solidarity and the bond of sisterhood. Incense and abundant perfume symbolized the beauty of heart and overflowing love, their fragrances to be spread over all the earth,[69] a reminder of Mary of Bethany's anointing of Jesus's feet during which "the house was filled with the fragrance of the perfume" (John 12:3).

Under the inspiration of Sister Evelyn and others, EWA created a structure for ongoing dialogue and work. The group held biennial conferences in addition to ongoing communication and dialogue. Following the theme of a "church of women themselves," EWA held meetings across the Asian continent. The 2002 Bangkok conference was followed by a virtual event in 2004 and in-person conferences in Yogyakarta in Indonesia, Colombo in Sri Lanka, Hua Hin in Thailand, Kuala Lumpur in Malaysia, Bangalore in India, Manila in the Philippines, and Ho Chi Minh City in Vietnam.

EWA today promotes publications by its members in an effort to include Asian women's voices in the canon of Catholic theology. As Dr. Mary Yuen explains in the documentary video, their aim is to move from "academics to liberation."[70] This liberation, according to Catholic social teachings like *Populorum Progressio,* must translate the gospel into the lives of the marginalized. For EWA, each human is sacred, and their full "integral development" is the goal and object of Catholic social mission. The women of EWA, under the inspiring vision of Sister Evelyn Monteiro and others, witness that the risen Christ lives among them—as a "people of his own who are zealous for good deeds" (Titus 2:14), indeed, as a "church of women themselves."

Sister Evelyn Monteiro, SCC, is the cofounder of Ecclesia of Women in Asia (EWA)—an association of Catholic women theologians in Asia—and vice president of the Indian Theologians Association. Monteiro was a faculty member and professor of systematic theology at Jnana-Deepa, Pontifical Institute of Philosophy and Theology at Pune, India, for many years, and visiting professor at other theological faculties in India and abroad. Monteiro has authored *Church and Culture: Communion in Pluralism* (2004) and edited several books and articles in national and international theological journals. She holds a doctorate in systematic theology from Centre Sèvres, Facultés jésuites de Paris, France.

11. SISTER NORMA PIMENTEL, MJ

WHILE POLITICAL COMMENTARIES on immigration swirl with innuendo, accusation, and demonizing, Sister Norma Pimentel responds with her adage, "Criticism of the bad is to do more of the good." Thus, her response to the "crisis" at the border is to be present with understanding, courage, and mercy. While the halls of Congress echo with vitriol, she and her colleagues are serving children and adults in search of shelter, food, and security. As executive director of Catholic Charities of Rio Grande Valley, Sister Norma works with her Catholic Charities staff, volunteers, and funders to help those caught between violence and oppression and walls and intolerance.

Sister Norma Pimentel has her feet, hands, and heart in three worlds: Mexico, the United States, and the reign of God. As a child she grew up in both the United States and Mexico. She was a daughter of Mexican immigrants, and spent her childhood years between Brownsville, Texas, and Matamoros, Mexico. Norma was raised primarily in Texas, awaiting finalization of her parents' immigration papers.

All three worlds come together in her work, for she labors to make God's reign a reality for those caught in the "no-persons" land between Mexico and the United States. In fact, her understanding of God's reign on earth inspires her work in Mexico and the United States. She stated, "Together we recognize that we have a responsibility. We are a people of God, people driven by the presence of God in ourselves and in others. When we see human suffering, we cannot turn our backs, we must respond."[71] She responds by recognizing the dignity conferred by God on every human person.

Pimentel is also a woman of prayer, prayer that moves heart and hands toward others. She told an interviewer that prayer is "key for who I am today and what I do," adding that if she "didn't make the time to wake up early in the morning to go to Mass and do my prayers and end with my prayers at night, I would get lost."[72]

At the border, Pimentel and Catholic Charities provide housing, pregnancy assistance, food, and counseling to people traumatized by dangerous treks from Central America through Mexico to the border. Seeking what we all want—security and dignity—these migrants have been robbed, beaten, manipulated, and preyed upon.

Catholic Charities has served hundreds of thousands of migrants in the last several years. Sister Norma has carried the good news of mercy around the world to open hearts to the needs of migrants. She speaks often before national and international audiences to "lift up our hearts" to the needs at the border. She has spoken at the United Nations and accompanied Pope Francis in 2017 as the Vatican launched Caritas Internationalis, "Share the Journey," to promote the culture of encounter. By emphasizing "encounter," Pope Francis, Sister Norma, and others seek to serve through proximity, presence, and dialogue.

Despite the anti-immigration rhetoric, many organizations seek to bring compassion to the complex reality of immigration. Many have recognized the courageous work of Sister Norma Pimentel and Catholic Charities. These acknowledgments include the Sister Margaret Cafferty Development of Peoples Award from the U.S. Bishops' Catholic Campaign for Human Development, the University of Notre Dame's prestigious Laetare Medal, Catholic Charities USA's "Keep the Dream Alive" award, and the Ignatian Solidarity Network

"Robert M Holstein, Faith Doing Justice Award." In 2015, Pope Francis personally thanked Pimentel for her work with immigrants in a virtual town hall meeting featured on ABC's *20/20*. That same year she was named one of *Our Sunday Visitor's* 2015 Catholics of the Year and won a nomination for "Texan of the Year." In 2019, she was one of *Fortune* magazine's "World's 50 Greatest Leaders." These awards are not accumulated for personal benefit; rather, they acknowledge that the day-to-day work to improve human life is a valued and necessary struggle.

Upon receiving any recognition, Sister Norma reminds her audiences of the dignity and needs of migrants, and that she is but one of many who serve those forgotten at the border. When she was named one of *Time* magazine's 100 Most Influential People in the world, her hope was that this will "bring more understanding and help people see more clearly what we can each do to respect all human life, especially the most vulnerable."[73]

Sister Norma's work among migrants did not begin at Catholic Charities. That position came following years of work delivering housing, counseling, and other services to those with no safe home or country. She had been one of the leaders of Casa Oscar Romero. The Casa was a refugee shelter in San Benito, and eventually Brownsville, for Central Americans fleeing war and poverty in the 1980s. Many were displaced by the U.S.-backed violence in El Salvador and Nicaragua, and the shelter provided emergency relief and temporary housing for hundreds of thousands of refugees.

Sister Norma often reminds her audiences that violence, corruption, and poverty are not the main obstacles to human dignity. The main obstruction, quoting Pope Francis, is the "globalization of indifference."[74] Indifference has two components, first, believing that the misery of others is not our problem, and second, that even if it is, we can't do anything about it. Pope Francis and Sister Pimentel call that a false narrative, for it is our problem, and we can do something about it.

> If you were to come to south Texas...if you have an opportunity to meet the families, you will find... they left their countries because they are afraid... of the violence....The families flee their country mostly to protect their children....If you get to know them, you will find out, they are not criminals. They are actually decent human beings.... They are here only because they want a chance at life, to take care of their families.[75]

12. SISTER HELEN PREJEAN, CSJ

SISTER HELEN PREJEAN is known by millions for her stand against the death penalty. Her 1993 publication, *Dead Man Walking,* was based on her correspondence with and eventual support for convicted murderer Elmo Patrick Sonnier. The book was on The New York Times Bestseller List for thirty-one weeks and was later made into an Academy Award–winning movie with the same title. Sister Helen met with Pope John Paul II and Pope Francis to urge them to update Catholic teaching to oppose legalized state murder. Her argument is not just that mercy should rule, but in many nations, in particular the United States, the death penalty is disproportionately applied to the poor, the Black, and the Brown.

When Sister Helen Prejean began her work on death row in the early 1990s, 50 percent of Americans supported the death penalty. By 2018, due to the work of Prejean and many others, 80 percent of Americans opposed murder by the state. Furthermore, in 2018 Pope Francis determined that executions were immoral and against Catholic social teaching. He noted, "The death penalty is unacceptable, an attack on the inviolability and dignity of the human person and contrary to the Gospel of Jesus Christ."[76] As a result of persistent interventions and advocacy by Sister Helen and others, as of 2019, 164 individuals on death row had won their freedom. They were found to have been wrongly identified and unjustly convicted; new evidence declared their innocence. After years of working for those on death row, Sister Helen expanded her vocation to include the families of victims. While some on death row are innocent, others have brought tremendous grief to the families of their victims. Sister Helen therefore started the group Survive, a support for those who must live with the grief of a murdered and beloved family member.

Sister Helen Prejean's work in America's death rows came slowly. Her autobiography, *River of Fire: My Spiritual Journey*, describes her life as an immersion in a blazing river where God's Spirit leads us to places we cannot foresee or fathom. She writes in the introduction:

> What it's always been about for me is the spiritual energy, the power that flows through us, lights us up, and enlivens whatever we touch, for me that energy has always been connected to God. Call it mystery, call it grace, call it the luminous center we touch sometimes and don't know what to call it, but we know its presence fills us with confidence and peace.[77]

Prejean's journey began as a child in Baton Rouge at a time when segregation was the law. Her parents employed Black house servants, and she noted in her autobiography that she did not have any relationships with African Americans as peers until she was forty-two years old.[78] For the first four decades of her life, Blacks were serving and bowing or were invisible.

Her early years of racial and social isolation continued after joining the Sisters of St. Joseph. Sister Helen joined the order in 1957 at eighteen years old. This era, after World War II and before Vatican II, was the apex of American Catholicism. People joined the priesthood and religious orders in record numbers. Ironically, the large numbers only increased "the Catholic ghetto" in which Catholic schools, neighborhoods, and parishes were sometimes separated from the world they were called to serve. Prejean writes about the enforced rigidity of pre–Vatican II convent life where friendships were discouraged and family visits forbidden. Prejean notes the main virtue was obedience: obedience to mother superior, the order, the bishop, and the pope. Critical thinking and engagement in social issues was forbidden, especially for women religious.

Much of this would soon change. In 1959, newly elected Pope John XXIII stunned the Catholic world with a call for the Second Vatican Council. In his opening address the pope proclaimed,

> Illuminated by the light of this Council, the Church —we confidently trust—will become greater in spiritual riches and, gaining the strength of new energies therefrom, she will look to the future without fear.[79]

He sought a fearless, stronger, updated church, capable of serving all humanity. These sentiments flowed into the documents of the Council and then out to the wider church. Prejean was among the millions impacted by this historic meeting; she noted that Vatican II and other movements in the church helped her discover "that God is glorified by persons truly alive, who make active use of intellect, imagination, and decisional power to do something exciting in the world."[80]

At the time of Vatican II, Sister Helen practiced the traditional roles of teaching and charity. She admits her past caused her to believe that Blacks were happy in their poverty, irresponsible in their sexual behavior, and incapable of managing their own affairs. Sister Marie Augusta, a sister of Notre Dame de Namur, led a retreat workshop for nuns that opened Sister Helen's heart and expanded her understanding of her Catholic mission. Sister Marie Augusta noted that in the Gospel of Mark,

> Jesus preached good news to the poor; integral to that good news is that the poor are to be poor no longer....Jesus was telling them...they have God's blessing to resist injustices that make their lives wretched. That their very dignity as sons and daughters of God calls them to strive for what is rightfully theirs. Justice, not charity. Active struggle, not passive compliance.[81]

That night, Sister Helen wrestled with the profound implications of Sister Marie's challenge, praying in desperation, "Who are you, Lord? What do you want me to do?"[82]

Sister Helen later joined Hope House in New Orleans, started by Sister Lory Schaff and the Sisters of Mercy in the heart of low-income housing projects. There the nuns listened to, empowered, and served the families, children, and elderly. Sister Helen learned much from Sister Lory, who often said, "Don't we believe in the one body of Christ? Why are we separating ourselves?"[83] Her experiences with Hope House led her to find Jesus in the faces of the poor. She wrote, "Now I'm learning that real praying means taking on other people's suffering as my own, and letting the experience rouse me to action."[84]

The "river of fire" continued to lead her to unexpected places. Sister Helen Prejean's ministry again expanded when she received a letter from Elmo Patrick Sonnier, a death row prisoner asking to correspond as his execution approached. What she thought would be a few exchanges of letters became a doorway into the lives of the damned. Her eyes opened to their humanity, their haunting traumas, their horrific crimes, and in some cases, their innocence. The callous system that condemned people, mostly poor, to death, and the inhuman nature of death row stunned her. She was shocked to learn that the states most likely to murder Black and poor defendants were the same states where slavery was legal for over two hundred years.

Sister Helen's encounter with Elmo Patrick Sonnier transformed her into one of the leading voices against the death penalty. Her immersion in the river of fire enabled her to see the humanity in the guilty, the unfairly judged, the victim, and the victim's families.

Reflecting on her journey, Sister Helen noted in *River of Fire* that once you answer the call, it never stops, that the current carries you farther than you ever imagined. Aware of how troubling and uncertain life can be, she reminds us of the words of St. John of the Cross: "When evening comes, you will be examined in love."[85] Sister Helen Prejean's book ends with an invitation to join her in the exhilarating, demanding, grace-filled journey in the river of fire.

PART II

LAYMEN AND LAYWOMEN

All the laity then, have the exalted duty of working for the ever greater extension of the divine plan of salvation to all people and every time and place.

The Dogmatic Constitution on the Church,
Lumen Gentium 33

Lay people ought themselves to take on as their distinctive tasks this renewal of the temporal order. Guided by the light of the Gospel and the mind of the church, prompted by Christian love, they should act directly in this domain and in their own way. As citizens...they must bring to their cooperation with others their own special competence, and act on their own responsibility; everywhere and always they have to seek the justice of the Kingdom of God.

Decree on the Apostolate of Lay People,
Apostolicam Actuositatem 1, 7

1. MARGUERITE BARANKITSE

WE OFTEN HEAR THAT COURAGEOUS acts of love are born in unspeakable horror and unimaginable violence. Marguerite (Maggie) Barankitse of Burundi exemplifies one who transformed tragedy and death into light and life.

Barankitse was born in southern Burundi, a Tutsi in a nation inhabited by both Hutu and Tutsi peoples. She became a teacher and over the years adopted seven children. Fully aware of the ongoing tension and conflicts between the Hutu and Tutsi peoples, she adopted children from both ethnic groups.

On October 24, 1993, Burundi's president Melchior Ndadaye was murdered by rampaging soldiers in a bloody coup. Ndadaye was a remarkable figure. As a Marxist, he sought to build class alliances among both Hutu and Tutsi, thus subsuming ethnic identity in favor of economic solidarity. He was also the first civilian and first Hutu president of Burundi, as well as the first to be democratically elected. Consequently, Ndadaye was a threat to those who benefited from instability and ethnic divisions. After Ndadaye's murder, Burundi was overwhelmed by violence, mayhem, and murder. Where Hutus were in the majority, Tutsis were attacked and massacred. In locations where Hutus were outnumbered, they were assaulted and killed by Tutsis. Both sides were inflamed by hate rhetoric and rumor, much like the massacres in neighboring Rwanda the following year.

Marguerite Barankitse was among the victims. When the violence broke out following Ndadaye's assassination, she took her seven children to the home of the Catholic bishop. Unfortunately, the Catholic bishop could offer little protection against the Tutsi mobs. Barankitse was beaten, stripped, tied up, and forced to watch as more than seventy people were murdered in front of her. Since she was Tutsi, she and her seven children were able to escape, along with other children she had hidden away.[1]

The unbridled hate she witnessed led not to paralysis but rather an outpouring of generosity, courage, and compassion. A deeply Catholic woman, she sought to demonstrate that love and forgiveness can overcome the worst manifestations of hate and cruelty. After the killings, she sought to create a place where Tutsi and Hutu could gather, converse, and live in peace.

Barankitse first reached out to international aid organizations, but they were busy with other efforts in Burundi. Undeterred, she went to the Catholic bishop, told him of her vision, and demanded land and food for her venture. She said if the church provided land and food, she and other volunteers and workers would provide courage, energy, and mercy.

She got the land and the food, and thus began the work of Maison Shalom, the "house of peace." In Maison Shalom, Hutu and Tutsi would live together in peace, sharing the same space, table, and life. In an interview she later said, "The Church gave us a piece of land and gradually we built little houses, began to farm, and built a small school. We took the name 'Shalom' because my children heard on the radio that *shalom* meant *peace,* and that is our dream."[2]

As the word of "peace" spread around Burundi, displaced children, orphans, the wounded, and families fleeing violence found a home at Maison Shalom. Her place of peace attracted not only those in need but also many who sought solutions to violence and division.

Her Catholic faith taught Barankitse that it is in giving that we receive, and thus at Maison Shalom, those who received help often themselves became members of the caring community. Barankitse noted that her goal was not to have an orphanage but a family. In addition, all were welcome: Tutsis and Hutus. Thus, Maison Shalom lived up to its name, a place of peace instead of hatred and division. She told an interviewer,

> We always try to create a family structure, with houses for children. And we always try to reintegrate children with their original families wherever possible. There are even some children who live with the families that killed their parents because they have been able to forgive.[3]

She added that Maison Shalom is more than food and shelter; it is a place of love that feeds the heart and a testimony that compassion can transform the ashes of war into hope and life.

Life from the ashes of war. Resurrection after crucifixion. Peace in the midst of violence. The community of peace continued to grow, and what was once a single house with a farm transformed a killing ground into a playground. In Maison Shalom are found counseling for rape victims, support for orphans, and healing for all.

The community also engaged in the political realm and advocated for the rights of refugee children. Barankitse and her staff worked to prevent recruitment of child soldiers. Maison Shalom served approximately twenty thousand children and youth and employed over 270 people, including nurses, psychologists, and educators. However, in 2015 the situation for Maison Shalom changed dramatically when Barankitse criticized the harmful policies of President Pierre Nkurunziza and joined youth demonstrations denouncing him.

Prophetic critiques of inhumane policies were not taken well, and Barankitse was forced to hide in an embassy in fear for her life. The government included her name on a list of people to be arrested and executed. She shortly fled to Rwanda, becoming like those she served, a refugee without a country. Displaced by not deterred, she founded the Oasis of Peace after settling in Rwanda. Following the model of Maison Shalom, the new project was a home for the homeless, working to serve some of the ninety thousand Burundian refugees in Rwanda. Barankitse later stated in an interview:

> I was already used to this work, and I knew education was one of the best ways to lift children out of despair. This is what led me to open "Oasis of Peace" a space where refugees can feel human again. We support children's education, we find scholarships for young refugees to attend university, we counsel victims of torture and rape, we teach refugees English so they can adapt in Rwanda's English-speaking society....Living in a refugee camp can crush you, but we want them to live in dignity, to transform displacement into an empowering experience. We also want to focus on building a culture of peace and forgiveness. We are building a new generation of leaders.[4]

Since girls and women often bear the brunt of an unstable and violent society, Marguerite worked to harness and elevate their talents. She noted in an interview:

> Women are candles in the darkness. Despite the challenges they live with, they stay strong.... Women also don't need to be taught much about peace, they instinctively understand the purpose

> of reconciliation, even after facing the worst atrocities....If you want to destroy the world, then you must destroy women. And nobody can do that. No matter how hard they try. We keep bouncing back and rising stronger than ever before.[5]

Marguerite Barankitse models the strength of women as survivors, problem solvers, and peacemakers. The examples of forgiveness and peace-making, and the reminder that God gives us strength to bounce back "stronger than before" are but a few of the enduring legacies of Marguerite Barankitse.

2. M. SHAWN COPELAND

THE BOSTON SCHOOL of Theology and Ministry held an event titled "Celebrating M. Shawn Copeland: Memory, Freedom and Solidarity" to honor the scholar's contributions to Black theology, Christian anthropology, social justice, and feminist theology. In the keynote address, School of Theology and Ministry associate professor Francine Cardman noted of Copeland that "the primary mode in which she does her scholarship and teaching is 'practical-political' theology, which connects the faith and life of Catholics and other Christians with the needs of the suffering, oppressed, and marginalized in the world."[6] Copeland weaves the Black experience into the Catholic response to suffering.

Dr. Copeland notes in the opening lines of her book *Knowing Christ Crucified: The Witness of African-American Religious Experience* that as a young child she once asked her grandmother, "Who is that man hanging from the cross?"[7] The answer to that question is now part of her life experience and her understanding of God's work in the world. "That man" for Copeland is not the helpless Victim or the predetermined "sacrifice" for our sins. "That man" is one who has shown us that the way to liberation and unity is through full immersion into the whole of human experience. Through the cross, Jesus is in full communion with the incarcerated, the outcast, and the rejected.

Copeland writes, "Francis of Assisi is reported to have said that the cross is a book. When we open that book in love and intelligence, we encounter traces of the crucified Jewish Jesus in human social suffering in our world."[8] Copeland reminds us that our encounter with the cross of Jesus is not a private relationship. Rather, when we "open the book" of the cross, we see God's love radically displayed and know that no human is beyond the reach of God. Our response to that love, according to Copeland, must be love. She also reminds us that intelligence, thoughtful reflection, and sound thinking are necessary as we "open the book." She urges us not to take lightly the meaning of the cross but to continually unearth its meaning by responding to love with love and the gift of intelligence.

M. Shawn Copeland opens the book of the cross for us through her lectures and writings. For Copeland, encountering the crucified Christ is transformative. She writes, "The Jewish Jesus of Nazareth forever changes our reception…of the human other, of humanity. For humanity is his concern, neither merely or incidentally, rather, humanity is his concern comprehensively, fully."[9] As a result of that encounter, she considers her theology, or study of God, as "practical-political theology." Copeland writes, "Practical-political theology in this context stands squarely before the cross of the crucified Jewish Jesus, that most mysterious meeting place of grace and freedom."[10]

Practical-political is fitting as it covers all of life. Practical ensures our faith makes a tangible difference in our daily life. Practical means theological reflection impacts our prayer life, family relations, interactions with others, and behavior at work, school, parish, and neighborhood. Political guarantees our faith is not divorced from the decisions, policies, institutions, -isms, and powers that impact our collective life in society. The political realm, often shunned for its compromises and messiness, is for Copeland a necessary entry point for the message of Jesus Christ. Her Black experience underscores the importance of the political, for she knows how political structures marred by racism and violence have undermined Black life.

Jesus's confrontation with the forces of destruction on our behalf calls us to respond in kind. Copeland writes, "And it is before the cross that the praxis of the Christian community must always be judged. For the cross exposes our pretense to personal innocence or neutrality."[11] Vocations, interests, and lifestyles must be viewed in light of the cross. She reminds us that commitment is not a once-and-for-all event but something we must uncover anew each day of our Christian journey. Before the cross we are not innocent and unaware of the suffering around us, nor can we afford the luxury of neutrality.

Copeland also asks us to live as her parish does when she writes, "Our 'church family' knows Christ crucified; we intentionally strive to grow in wisdom and grace, knowledge and courage, in order to struggle against injustice."[12] Again, the cross is not an abstraction or an irrelevant religious fantasy. It is rooted in human solidarity and a love without boundaries, all expressed in the liturgy and practice of the local parish.

Following this path of unity and love, M. Shawn Copeland has served with the Felician Sisters for six years, twenty-one years with the Adrian Dominicans, and had a career as a theologian, lecturer, mentor, teacher, scholar, and author. Her impact on Black Catholic life in America is deep and wide. Copeland served as staff to the National Black Sisters Conference in their early years, she and Rev. Muhammad Kenyatta formed the first Black Ecumenical Consultation, and she is considered one of the foremost Black Catholic theologians in the nation. She acknowledges that her studies of Bernard Lonergan's teachings on faith, theological method, insight, and the human good grounded her theology and practice. Copeland also notes the enduring influence of Johann Baptist Metz, James Cone, and Gustavo Gutiérrez. Copeland credits the influence of Barbara Kaczmarek for teaching her to treasure her relationship with Jesus Christ and take seriously the study and implications of theology.

From her days as a child when she asked, "Who is that man hanging on the cross?," M. Shawn Copeland's aim has been to help us know Christ crucified and to continually open the book of the cross so that our practical and political life is shaped by love and human solidarity.

Her influence spans the academy, the parish, and society at large. Professor Copeland taught theology at St. Norbert College, Yale University Divinity School, Marquette University, and the Institute for Black Catholic Studies, Xavier University. She is recognized as one of the most important influences in North America in drawing attention to issues surrounding African American Catholics.

Copeland has also served as convener of the Black Catholic Theological Symposium (BCTS), an interdisciplinary association of Black Catholic scholars. She was the first African American and first African American woman to serve as president of the Catholic Theological Society of America (CTSA), the primary professional association of more than one thousand Catholic theologians in the United States and Canada. She has served the American Academy of Religion (AAR) as co-chair of the Program Unit on Women and Religion, a member of the Steering Committees of the Womanist Approaches to Religion and Society Group as well as the Black Theology Group, and a member of the Grant Committee on Research Proposals.

In all of these capacities, M. Shawn Copeland asks that we know Christ crucified, and through that "knowing," utilize our practical theology to bring the love and justice of Jesus to all our relationships, commitments, and values.

Copeland's voice is one that is indefatigable, fighting to show those who say they love God how they have failed to love their neighbor....Theologizing from the treatment of Black women's bodies historically through chattel slavery to the present, Shawn raised the alarm—for the church at large, and for the Catholic Church in particular—that failing to address theologically the questions of race and gender and poverty and oppression, was a failure to serve God rightly.[13]

3. DR. LENA EDWARDS, OSF

LENA FRANCIS EDWARDS was an African American born in Washington, DC, in 1900, on the Feast of St. Francis. Separated by seven centuries, another language, and a distant continent, Lena Edwards nevertheless followed the teachings of the well-known saint. Lena's mother was Catholic and instilled in Lena and her three siblings a love of the faith, a sense of purpose, and a calling to serve others.

Lena took this calling to heart. Graduating as valedictorian from Washington, DC's Dunbar High School in 1917, she attended Howard University for undergraduate studies and graduated from their School of Medicine in 1924. She went to historically Black Howard University instead of a white college because "I knew who I was and was proud of it...I didn't want to go to one of those schools and come back brainwashed."[14] She and her husband, Dr. Keith Madison, later moved to Jersey City, New Jersey. Despite her education and talent, Edwards, as a Black female doctor, confronted two almost insurmountable obstacles, gender and race. Her application to several hospitals was cast aside in favor of white male candidates. Undaunted, she opened her own obstetrical-gynecological clinic in her home. Dr. Edwards served local poor and working-class families from her clinic for the next twenty years. When she noticed the difference between "poor man's treatment vs. rich man's treatment," she decided to again try to join the hospital staff to lift the quality of care to the poor.[15] Utilizing her university education and clinical experience, she eventually gained residency at the local hospital. Similar to the focus of her clinic,

Dr. Edwards encouraged and provided quality care for the poor of Jersey City. She often chided her white peers who appeared to provide better health services to the wealthy.

Dr. Edwards's vocation was not confined to the clinic or the hospital; she visited schools, churches, and neighborhoods in Jersey City to advocate for quality women's health services regardless of income. During this era, she was one of the nation's few female OB-GYN doctors, and her race and gender provided a particular sensitivity to those often excluded from quality care. Motherhood was not a theory for her, for she had six children of her own. Between her clinic and the hospital, Dr. Edwards delivered over five thousand babies in her career. Countless poor and working-class mothers received better and perhaps life-saving care from Dr. Edwards. She also helped organize the People's Charitable League in Jersey City. The league operated a daycare center for working families who otherwise could not afford childcare. After her clinic work, Dr. Edwards would frequently end her days with a visit to the daycare center to provide the mothers with helpful medical advice.

Despite her education, clinic, hospital experience, community advocacy, and volunteer work, year after year Dr. Lena Edwards was denied her OB-GYN board certification. While white male doctors with less experience and certainly less empathy were certified, Dr. Edwards was bypassed. When her application was finally approved, she became one of the first African American women to be OB-GYN board certified.[16]

In 1954, after thirty years providing health care to all, particularly the poor, Lena Edwards returned to the classroom to teach obstetrics at the Howard University School of Medicine. While in Washington, DC, she served the poor through the Urban League, the National Association of Colored Women's Clubs, the Social Work Advisory Committee, and the Catholic International Council. Dr. Edwards also served on the boards of a home for unwed mothers and a local maternal welfare organization.

Dr. Edwards's service was rooted in her faith. A lifetime Catholic, she felt the call to a deeper spiritual life in the 1940s. Following prayer, reflection, and discernment, she became a Third Order Secular Franciscan. Married people with secular jobs and other commitments could join this order provided they practiced the teachings of simplicity and prayer in their daily lives. In many respects Dr. Edwards's life already reflected elements of the Franciscan "Gospel Way of Life," and her participation as a Third Order Franciscan enhanced her service to humanity through faith in Christ.

In 1959, Dr. Edwards moved to Hereford, Texas, where migrant workers lived in an old military barracks without basic sanitation facilities and health care. Drawing on her years of experience, she set up a fifteen-bed maternity hospital with donated materials and financial contributions. Her small hospital was not equipped for the more serious cases, so she used her board certification to get her patients into the closest hospital. In a community where many infants died at birth, Dr. Edwards and her colleagues dramatically reduced infant mortality in Hereford. There are many families alive today whose parents or grandparents would have died without the intervention of Dr. Lena Edwards.

In 1964, during the civil rights movement and the War on Poverty, President Lyndon Johnson awarded Dr. Lena Edwards the Presidential Medal of Freedom.[17] This award, the U.S. government's highest peacetime honor, publicly recognized the work of Dr. Edwards, a Black woman who overcame racism, sexism, and discrimination to save the lives of hundreds for whom health care was unaffordable.

A 1966 heart attack forced her to leave Hereford and return to New Jersey for recuperation. Not yet done with "bearing fruit," while "resting" she worked with organizations to detect and prevent uterine cancer and provide free medical care to low-income seniors. In 1967, she received the Poverello Medal in recognition of a life lived in conformity with the teachings of St. Francis of Assisi.[18] Edwards's commitment to God and the Franciscan order on behalf of the poor continued until her death in Lakewood, New Jersey, in 1986.

Her legacy lives on, not only in the lives she saved but also in the Jersey City charter school named after her, dedicated to academic excellence and the development of ethical values. The Dr. Lena Edwards Charter School recognizes her academic accomplishments, her compassionate service to the people of Jersey City, and her faith in action.

4. DR. PAUL FARMER

DOCTOR, ANTHROPOLOGIST, AUTHOR, global health expert, and, some say, saint, Paul Farmer died unexpectedly on February 21, 2022. Farmer and his collaborators confronted some of the world's most challenging health conditions and realized that abject poverty contributes to and intensifies poor health. In response, they created Partners In Health, a global organization formed to address poor health and poverty through compassion, partnering, and medical expertise. Partners In Health (PIH) was founded in 1987 by Dr. Paul Farmer, Ophelia Dahl, Dr. Jim Yong Kim, Tom McCormack, and Tom White. Dr. Kim remembers at their founding that Paul Farmer suggested, "Let's start a nonprofit with only one rule: everybody has to be kind. We have to agree to practice unconditional kindness."[19]

PIH's mission is "to provide a preferential option for the poor in health care."[20] The organization partners with impoverished communities to care for the most neglected people on earth. From Haiti's slums to Rwanda's rice fields, Partners In Health engages with the poor as equals in dignity and responsibility. By establishing long-term relationships with sister organizations based in settings of poverty, Partners In Health strives to achieve two overarching goals. They work to bring modern medicinal science to those most in need of it and "to serve as an antidote to despair." PIH's website states, "We refuse to accept that any life is worth less than another," and it sets forth the belief that "injustice has a cure."[21] Since its founding, Partners In Health and its collaborators have saved, prolonged, and improved millions of lives in some of the poorest parts of the world.

In high school and college, Paul Farmer was a brilliant student whose future was considered by most as full of promise and personal achievement. When he attended Duke University, fellow fraternity brother and future Jesuit priest John Dear remembered he was a popular student and hosted some of the best parties on campus.

What changed, that a popular, brilliant student set aside personal comfort for a life of service to others? Dr. Paul Farmer speaks of three incidents that shifted his priorities. First was the 1980 murder of Archbishop Oscar Romero. In a *National Catholic Reporter* article his friend John Dear writes, "He underwent a dramatic conversion on the night Archbishop Oscar Romero was killed in El Salvador."[22] Farmer attended a prayer vigil for the martyred archbishop, and Dear remembers, "He told me, he suddenly realized that to be a Christian meant you had to serve Christ on the side of the poor."[23] Farmer was raised Catholic, but at that time the Gospel was not the defining ethic of his life. Bishop Romero's murder showed him that following Christ could put the believer at odds with the prevailing culture. Years later, Farmer's chief advisor Jennie Weiss Block, OP, noted that Romero's death "gave him new interest and respect for the faith of his childhood, and a home for his yearnings to serve."[24]

The next transformative incident in his life was his encounter with Belgian nun, Sister Julianna DeWolf. They met when Farmer chose to research and analyze the conditions of migrant workers in North Carolina as a college project. He witnessed firsthand Sister Julianna's devotion to being with, learning from, and empowering migrant families. Farmer often referred to Sister Julianna as "the social justice nun." Further, the study enabled him to confront the "contrast experience," noting the difference between pampered campus life and impoverished migrant camps.

The third influence was his encounter with the writings of Father Gustavo Gutiérrez, OP, the Peruvian "father" of liberation theology. Gutiérrez, a pastor to the poor and a theologian in the academy, understood the good news of Jesus Christ as a holistic liberation of the poor from diminished life on the margins. He understood God's call to Christians as having a "preferential option for the poor," later a driving theme for Partners In Health. Years after reading his work, Farmer met Gutiérrez, and they often participated on the same panel discussions regarding their respective vocations. Gutiérrez would later say that Farmer and Partners In Health are examples of liberation theology in practice.[25]

These three events reinforced Farmer's study of medicine as a vehicle to serve. While still in his medical studies, Paul Farmer moved to Haiti, where he lived in a small house in a squatter settlement. He would live in that home for several more years, and during that time he worked with the community to build a school and a hospital.

The vision for Partners In Health evolved into an organization that continues to improve the lives of the poor across the globe. One anecdote summarizes the daily impacts of PIH. Farmer was once attending to a young woman who was seriously ill with an infectious disease. Without intervention, the disease would be terminal. When Farmer asked where her father was, she told him he was at home, in tears, building a coffin for her burial. A few days later, as she responded to medical treatment, Farmer told the woman, "Tell your father to get rid of the coffin; you are not going to need it."[26]

Thousands have been given new life through the ministry of Partners In Health. Whether confronting tuberculosis in Haiti, cholera in Rwanda, Ebola in Liberia, or illnesses in Peru, Partners In Health has worked alongside the poor for better health. Empowering the poor was central to Farmer's commitment, often recalling that Jesus empowered people to take part in their own healing when he proclaimed, "Your faith has saved you."

Farmer was also chair of Global Health and Social Medicine at Harvard University, a renowned expert on global health, an anthropologist, an author, and a UN deputy special envoy to Haiti. A typical schedule could include a morning lecture at Harvard Medical School, an afternoon flight to Haiti, evening PIH work in Haiti, and a morning flight to serve in Rwanda. Farmer also found time to write, publishing *Pathologies of Power; Fevers, Feuds and Diamonds: Ebola and the Ravages of History;* and many other books.

Dr. Farmer often said our world is connected both for good and for ill. This struck home to him when he learned that the bullets found after massacres of El Salvadoran peasants were stamped, "Lake City, Missouri." The bullet makers in Missouri joined the El Salvadoran military to bring about death. In contrast, Dr. Paul Farmer, the founders of PIH, and their workers and partners came together to bring hope, good health, and new life to those most in need. Dr. Farmer often reminded his audiences that there is not a first world, or a third world, but only one that we all share in common. He said:

> Unless we link our spirituality to justice and to the good works we know to be necessary in a world in which a billion people go without adequate food, clean water, health care, and a modicum of justice, we will have, as was noted two thousand years ago, nothing but dead faith.[27]

5. ELISABETH SCHÜSSLER FIORENZA

THE TITLES OF ELISABETH SCHÜSSLER Fiorenza's books are a window into her theological commitment. For example, in her book *Jesus: Miriam's Child, Sophia's Prophet?* Jesus is not merely the male "Son of God" but the human child of Miriam who came to proclaim the message of Sophia from the Hebrew Scriptures. According to Fiorenza, the ministry and message of Jesus is grounded in the faith of his mother. It was she, Miriam of Nazareth, who proclaimed during the Visitation with her older cousin Elizabeth, "The Mighty One has done great things for me....He has...lifted up the lowly; he has filled the hungry with good things" (Luke 1:49, 52–53).

Fiorenza also argues that the good news Jesus brought echoes Holy Wisdom, Sophia of the Hebrew Scriptures.

> For she is the breath of the power of God, and a pure emanation of the glory of the Almighty...for she is a reflection of eternal light, a spotless mirror of the working of God...while remaining in herself, she renews all things; in every generation she passes into holy souls, and makes them friends of God, and prophets. (Wis 7:25–27)

Miriam's Son, Sophia's prophet, Jesus, came so that we, too, can become friends of God and cocreators of a new and better world.

In the theology of Fiorenza, the man Jesus is not the forerunner of an all-male priesthood, the male Son of God, or the embodiment of holy masculinity. Jesus instead was incarnate as a human being, and under the guidance of Miriam and the energy of Sophia, liberates us all, women and men, to our full humanity.

For Fiorenza, theology is rooted in the God of life and love, and thus everything is interpreted in that light. Whether the man Jesus, holy scripture, Vatican teachings, or the meaning of the sacraments, the God of life is the center. This perspective is evident in her 2007 Eugene M. Burke, CSP Lecture on Religion and Society titled, "The Power of the Word: Scripture and the Rhetoric of Empire."[28] These lectures are in honor of Passionate priest, theologian, church historian, and ecumenist Father Eugene Burke.

Fiorenza's lecture argues that God's word is inherently powerful and yet requires a feminist perspective to fully express its meaning. She tells the audience that feminism, "the F-word," is "the radical notion that women are people." With this foundation, she teaches that a reading of scripture through a feminist lens uncovers a God different from what we have heard of over the last two millennia. She says that "women are not wives, handmaids or beasts of burden," but are "full decision-making citizens." Thus, as wise, articulate, functioning, and self-determined human beings, women are empowered to understand God and study scripture from their experience, values, and insight.

Furthermore, since men have used legal, economic, and physical power to dominate women for centuries, Fiorenza studies scripture to understand the dynamics of power in human relations. She maintains that much of scripture was written by elite men in the context of various forms of empire. Consequently, a sacred text must be analyzed from what it has to say about power relationships. Specifically, she tells us the texts that buttress the rhetoric of empire or male domination often convey a "power over." "Power over" includes language and practice about domination, submission, and subordination. Since imperial or patriarchal systems of domination require violence to sustain unequal relations, in some cases scripture condones or justifies force and conquest of the other.

She maintains that one task for feminist theologians is to recognize and critique the power relationships in scripture. The second task, she argues, is that the feminist reading of scripture must locate and reflect on a different power, that is, the "power to." Diametrically opposed to "power over," "power to" in the scriptures empowers us to overcome oppression, live in community, and resist exploitation. In uncovering the "power to" of sacred scripture, the reader, indeed, the entire discerning community, can hear and unleash God's creative energy for a new and better world.

It is only when we discern the "power to" that we are empowered by the word of God to confront empire in faithfulness and courage. Since God is the God of life and all humans are created in the image of God, any scripture that empowers and dignifies all humans is of God. Any scripture that does not empower and dignify must be seen as not from God. In a statement contrary to literal biblical interpretations, she said, "We recognize the Bible contains revelation, but not all scripture is revelation" from God.

Her understanding of God as a Divine Presence devoted above all else to human flourishing enables her to locate God's truth of liberation in the sacred text. For Fiorenza, the scriptures that sanction misogyny, war, violence, or slavery are not from God. She, like the woman seeking the lost coin in Luke 15, searches carefully for the word of the God of human dignity and freedom.

Her reading of scripture also speaks of the church, the *ekklesia*, as a radical democratic society that unearths divine wisdom in our collective struggle for human dignity. Fiorenza tells us that scripture does not express a message "given once for all time, or engraved in tablets of stone." Rather, reading and reflecting on the scriptures in light of God's love for humanity opens us to a lifetime of growth. She notes, "The power of sacred Scripture is that it gives the nourishment of divine wisdom to struggle against empire and exploitation in our daily lives." This word from God to his beloved people "does not require obedience and acceptance, but is a power to, and source of creativity, courage and solidarity."[29]

The task of feminist theologians and practitioners is to listen carefully to what the Spirit says through both the scriptures and their experience. She reminds us to move beyond the "power over" passages that contrast with our experience of the God of love and learn from the words that give us "power to." Anything, whether scripture, teaching, or practice, that promotes violence or domination is contrary to God and must be rejected. On the other hand, any scripture, teaching, or practice that honors the human person is from God and must be both accepted and practiced in our lives.

God's word, according to Fiorenza, is not fixed but is the creative energy required in our ongoing struggle to create the radically democratic community that God intends. She also reminds us that we discern the Holy Spirit in our world through active work. That Spirit, as evident from the life of Jesus, is not a disembodied abstract event but is manifest in our commitment to create a radical democratic community in the midst of empire and exploitation.

Fiorenza's biblical insights arise from a lifetime of exploring the sacred texts. As a student and later professor of theology, she has been a pioneer in biblical interpretation and feminist theology. She has also taught biblical and theological epistemology, hermeneutics, rhetoric, the politics of interpretation, and theological education, radical equality, and democracy.

Fiorenza is cofounder of the *Journal of Feminist Studies in Religion,* founding coeditor of *Concilium,* and was the first woman president of the Society of Biblical Literature. As teacher, author, lecturer, and mentor, Elisabeth Schüssler Fiorenza has transformed the perspectives and vocations of many women and men applying theology to politics, economics, and society.

Her many books, articles, essays, and lectures lift women's voices to their rightful place on earth. Half of humanity has been silenced, marginalized, and exploited for centuries, and Fiorenza utilizes their wisdom to recover God's message from the distortion of domination to be a source of liberation.

6. DIANA HAYES

FOR CATHOLIC SCHOLAR Diana Hayes, intellectual pursuits are but an avenue to illuminate the practical application of theology to everyday life. Grounded in the bitter realities of Black female life in the American South, her theology was never theoretical. It is, rather, reflections on the nature of God in the tapestry of our daily living. She imbued her personal reflections with intellectual rigor. Hayes obtained a Juris Doctor from the George Washington University National Law Center and gained licentiate in sacred theology from the Catholic University of America. She is the first African American woman in history to receive the Pontifical Doctor of Sacred Theology degree (STD) from the Catholic University of Louvain (Belgium).

Much of her studies explored the work of the founder of Black theology, James Cone. Cone stunned the Christian world with the 1968 publication of *Black Theology and Black Power.* Despite persistent criticism and opposition, Cone followed that groundbreaking work with *A Black Liberation of Theology, God of the Oppressed,* and *The Cross and the Lynching Tree.* As a Black Catholic woman, Hayes expanded Cone's contributions by including womanist insights in Cone's Black theology.

Weaving together Cone's work, Black theology, Catholic social thought, and the Black female experience in America, Dr. Hayes has made significant contributions to faith and praxis. She taught courses in liberation, womanist, and Black theologies, contextual theologies, religion and public life, and African American and womanist spirituality for years at

Georgetown University, the Oblate School of Theology, and Xavier University's (Louisiana) Institute for Black Catholic Studies. She is a member of the Black Catholic Theological Symposium.

Hayes's work was not restricted to the university or the academic world. Her lectures, books, interviews, articles, and speeches inject the breadth of her theological reflections into issues of race, misogyny, injustice, and inequality. A prolific lecturer and writer, she has published, among other works, *Standing in the Shoes My Mother Made: A Womanist Theology; Forged in the Fiery Furnace: African-American Spirituality; No Crystal Stair: Womanist Spirituality; Hagar's Daughters: Womanist Ways of Being in the World; Were You There: Stations of the Cross; Trouble Don't Last Always: Soul Prayers; And Still We Rise: An Introduction to Black Liberation Theology.*

Hayes's books, articles, and essays depict God as a liberator, a defender of human dignity, and a lover of all humanity, loving particularly, but not exclusively, those forced to the margins. In a 2018 lecture at the Oblate School of Theology about her book *Standing in the Shoes My Mother Made*, she stated, "To be born black and female in the Old South was to be born into a life of struggle, hardship and limitation."[30] She noted that despite little formal education, her mother was the most intelligent person she had ever known. Hayes recounted that her mother had wisdom grounded in daily experiences of oppression, disrespect, and hardship. Raised in the rural outskirts of Chattanooga, Tennessee, Hayes recalled her mother as deprived of an education but wise in the ways of life. She noted that

> like many women, unable because of their limited circumstances to live the lives they would choose for themselves, she prepared her daughters and countless others, male and female, for a future she

> knew nothing about. She and our other "sheroes" of faith somehow prepared, and provided us with whatever it was that we needed to survive.... Somehow they knew what we needed to exist and persist in the new world aborning, even though they themselves more than likely would never see that world.[31]

However, the wisdom of her mother could not always overcome racism, inequality, enforced poverty, poor schools, and other injustices. Dr. Hayes said those obstacles created "a hemorrhage" referring to the drain of human potential. By using a term reserved medically for the "escape of blood from a ruptured blood vessel, especially when profuse," Hayes graphically illuminated the talents and gifts lost to humanity through the crimes of racism.

As a Catholic, a woman, and a scholar, her allusion also recalls the story of the woman in the Gospels who suffered from hemorrhages for twelve years. In the fifth chapter of Mark, the writer recounts, "She had heard about Jesus, and came up behind him in the crowd and touched his cloak, for she said, 'If I but touch his clothes, I will be made well'" (Mark 5:27–28). In similar fashion, Hayes's theology seeks to enable hemorrhaging people to reach out and touch the healing presence of Jesus Christ.

In many respects, Diana Hayes's Oblate lecture summarizes her vocation: first, to describe, highlight, and uncover all those forces that diminish human potential and well-being, and second, to show us how reaching out and "touching" Jesus can begin our empowerment and healing.

In a 2002 *America* magazine interview, Diana Hayes was asked to name her favorite book. She responded with *The Divided Mind of the Black Church: Theology, Piety and Public Witness* by Rev. Raphael Warnock.[32] Diana Hayes said:

> I chose this work because of its emphasis on the need for dialogue between theologians and the church, pastors and parishioners alike. Many of the issues raised are applicable not only for blacks in the Catholic Church but for other Catholics who still find themselves marginalized. Black and womanist theologies are still little known in the Catholic community and their solidarity with feminist, mujerista, Asian, Native American, Latino/a and other theologians is still overlooked. This work encourages all of those historically marginalized in our church and others who find themselves increasingly marginalized, such as gays and women in general, to work in solidarity to overcome the divide between personal piety and social justice that threatens the stability and viability of the universal Catholic Church.[33]

Her work to overcome the divide between personal piety and social justice resonates with her lifetime commitment to link academic theology with the real lives of people in struggle. Diana Hayes and other Black Catholic scholars, religious, priests, bishops, and laypeople carry within them important gifts of the Holy Spirit to edify the church, empower humanity, and build the common good. As the Second Letter to Timothy asks that he "stir up the gift" within him, (1:6), may we as the People of God stir up the gifts of Black Catholics like scholar Diana Hayes.

7. MONIKA HELLWIG

ONE OF THE IRONIES OF Catholicism is that scholars and theologians often considered "heretical" by the hierarchy are among those most committed to recovering the roots of authentic Catholic tradition. Theologian Monika Hellwig, often at odds with the Vatican, is but one example. Hellwig did not accept church doctrine and teachings without a thorough examination of the ancient roots of the faith. In an address to the Catholic Theological Society, she once noted that many are doing "instant theology" and neglecting the cumulative wisdom of the past. For her, "instant theology" was a theologically lazy way of substituting our personal preferences and political ideologies for sound theological reflection and practice.

This was not her way. Hellwig believed the way forward was to absorb and expand upon centuries of cumulative spiritual wisdom, based on one's own intellect, gifts, and experience. As a refugee from the Nazis, a nun, a medical missionary, a poet, a theologian, a mother, a servant, a prayer leader, and the executive director of the Association of Catholic Colleges and Universities, she melded theological reflection with the real world of suffering and struggle.

Born in Germany before World War II to a Dutch mother, a German father, and Jewish grandparents, the family moved to Holland after Hitler came to power. When Germany invaded Holland, the Nazis killed her father, and Monika and her two sisters were taken in by a family in Scotland and provided a home and place of love and support. This experience showed Monika that in the midst of death, separation, and grief, love and mercy still flourish.

In the 1950s, Monika moved to the United States and later joined the religious order of the Medical Mission Sisters. She served in Washington, DC, and Philadelphia for several years, and in 1962 the sisters sent her to be a correspondent at the Second Vatican Council. In that role, Monika Hellwig was one of the few women who were privy to the inner workings of the bishops as they grappled with the transformative documents of the Council.

As she listened and reported on the bishops' discussions on the direction of the Church, she found herself called to the laity. She came to believe, as the Council taught, that baptism confers both dignity and calling on the laity. *Lumen Gentium*, the Dogmatic Constitution on the Church, described the role of the laity in the world:

> It is the special vocation of the laity to seek the Kingdom of God by engaging in temporal affairs and directing them according to God's will....There they are called by God to contribute to the sanctification of the world from within....Thus...they manifest Christ to others. (31)

These words, prayers, and reflections led Monika Hellwig to leave the Medical Mission Sisters and pursue a life engaged in the world as a layperson. Her experience and education opened the way for her to become a theologian and teacher at Georgetown University. Well-respected for her lectures and insights, Monika was considered by many students to be a mentor and a guide.

For Hellwig as for the liberation theologian Gustavo Gutiérrez, sound theology was simply reflection on your life of praxis. In her work *The Mandalas Do Not Break: A Theological Autobiographical Essay,* she wrote:

> "Theology is the critique of praxis." When I first read these words in an essay by Gustavo Gutierrez, I recognized them immediately as a description of my own experience. Christian theology is the critique of the praxis of trying to live by the gospel of Jesus Christ within a constantly changing world. Catholic theology is the critique of the praxis of doing it within the Catholic community and its traditions. Following this line of thought one also comes to the realization that there is a...lay theology...feminine theology...a theology of the uprooted...a theology that springs again and again from the bitterly oppressed and overwhelms us from time to time in our comfortable entrenchments.[34]

Her praxis would later include the vocation of motherhood. In the midst of race riots, assassinations of Black political leaders, and racial divisions, Monika Hellwig adopted and raised three African American children. Most certainly her theology took on the consuming and practical demands of family and raising children.

From 1996 until 2005, Monika Hellwig was president and executive director of the Association of Catholic Colleges and Universities. In this role she urged the church to translate its theological insights into acts of justice, to respond to real social needs, and question anything that did not advance human flourishing. When the Vatican tried to enforce "orthodox" and conservative perspectives in Catholic universities, she countered with tolerance, discussion, and debate. She insisted on teaching critical thinking, not static dogma. For example, she led the stand against the Vatican's censure of Rev. Charles Curran of Catholic University for his opposition to church teachings on abortion and gays and lesbians. The society called Curran's punishment dangerous, professionally incomprehensible, and unjust.

For her work among students, her contributions toward a theology that acts and liberates, and her stand against Vatican sanctions, Monika Hellwig was often called, "the People's Theologian." She urged her students to continually form and advance their theology from their concrete action in the world. Thus, for many, theology became not an abstract collection of theories about God but an expansive faith grounded in action and theological reflections on the struggle for justice.

Monika Hellwig did not confine her work to the university and the classroom. She founded the Christian Life Community (CLC) at Georgetown University for discussion, prayer, and support, and was an active member of St. Rose of Lima parish in Gaithersburg, Maryland.

In 1987 she delivered the Presidential Address for the Catholic Theological Society, titled "The Role of the Theologian in Today's Church."[35] Well remembered for its remarkable insights, the presentation asserted that theologians are to be myth makers who uncover God's truth, fools who challenge prejudices, builders of an empowering and constructive theology, archivists who treasure the wisdom of the past, critics who call us to what is good, and ghosts whose insights are assimilated while they themselves are forgotten.[36]

Monika would often remind friends, students, and audiences of the importance of prayer. Upon receiving the *Populorum Progressio* Award, she wrote that while often despair can lead us to conclude that "it is beyond our scope to act, and that our only contribution can be prayer[,]...prayer itself is...for our own transformation and empowerment by grace to live…and act according to the wisdom of the Reign of God."[37] In 1993, recalling her previous twenty years as a Catholic scholar and theologian, she noted in a lecture:

> In my journey…as a Catholic scholar what have I really learned? First of all, we cannot keep the Holy Spirit out of the church, no matter how much we try to domesticate the whole enterprise. Secondly, that the church is wiser…when it listens to many voices. Thirdly, that we are the bearers of tradition and shapers of it for the future….Fourthly never to be afraid of the truth, but to seek the truth with humility and faith and the readiness to be proved wrong and to begin the search again. Fifthly, that conflict is part of growth and the shaping of tradition, but that hatred and rejection of those who differ need not be. And last, that as educated Catholics…we are part of a very important intellectual contribution to our society and to the world—a contribution that is an integral component of the redemption.[38]

8. JACQUES MARITAIN

JACQUES MARITAIN MET Raissa Ousmanoff, the daughter of Jewish immigrants to France, at the Sorbonne University in Paris in 1903. The two were desperately searching for the meaning of life, and their common quest brought them together. Jacques and Raissa found the intellectual activity on Paris's Left Bank empty and lacking, and frustrated by the emptiness of life and the absence of purpose and hope, Jacques and Raissa were in despair. They were so desperate for relief that they entered into a suicide pact if they could not find some reason to hope.

Their friend, the poet and religious thinker Charles Péguy, urged them to attend lectures by philosopher Henri Bergson. Soon Jacques and Raissa were enthralled with Bergson's musings on creativity, intuition, and the power of free will. Revived by Bergson's insights, the two married and committed themselves to finding and sharing life-affirming truths. Philosophy was not their only source of insight, and shortly after marriage, they joined the Catholic Church, attracted by the depth of Catholic spirituality.

Maritain looked often to Thomas Aquinas (1225–74), the saint who fused Aristotle's philosophy with reasoned principles to arrive at faith in God and an understanding of human existence. For Maritain, Aquinas's insights were essential in locating God and our role in the world. Often Thomism, or the thought of Thomas Aquinas, is associated with rigid medieval thinking. Through the lens of Jacques Maritain, Aquinas's teachings promote the dignity of the human person, human rights, and positive action in the world by believers. Scholars note that Maritain's writings influenced Thomas Merton, the Rev. Dr. Martin Luther King Jr., Saul Alinsky, Popes John XXIII and Paul VI, and many others.

From 1945 to 1948, Maritain served as the French ambassador to the Vatican. Through his application of Thomist thought to the modern world, he reaffirmed the dignity of the human person and the renewed focus on human rights in the aftermath of World War II. His insights were instrumental in the development of the Universal Declaration of Human Rights adopted by the United Nations in 1948. In addition, his focus on the importance of political engagement informed the work of the Christian democratic parties in Western Europe and on constitutions in Latin America. His influence is also evident in the Canadian Charter of Rights and Freedom and the Constitution of the Fourth French Republic.

Many of his books attempted to make philosophical truths available to laypeople, particularly *Degrees of Knowledge* and *Introduction to Philosophy*. In *Introduction to Philosophy*, he attempted to demonstrate that God could be known through faith and through reason and philosophical thinking. Some consider his shortest volume, *The Person and the Common Good*, as his most significant.

In this book he affirms that our liberty, our ability to make rational choices, and our capacity to understand the mysteries of the universe enable us to grasp and transcend the stars and the world of nature. He also writes that through contemplation, we are bound to God in a special way. Maritain considers contemplation the most important and primary vocation of the human person, for it is there we encounter our deepest self and the God who created us. He taught that our encounter with God through contemplation represents the highest good we can attain, and that no other human activity compares with this relationship with the Divine. He wrote, "Contemplative activity is the highest of human activities...because it binds man to God."[39]

Although union with God is our highest calling, Maritain wrote that it is not the end goal of the spiritual life. He notes that the virtues we absorb from contemplation must flow back into our lives and be visible in our relationships, vocations, and activities in the world. Union with the Divine is the foundation of our work for the common good. That work, emerging from our participation in the life of God, is an urgent necessity. Maritain argues that the suffering, misery, and violence in the world must be met with the love we encounter in God.

When discussing the common good, Maritain lists tangible ways to enhance the dignity of every human person, including just laws, living traditions, cultural treasures, and financial stability. He writes:

The common good includes all these things, and much more besides—something more profound, more concrete and more human....It includes...civic conscience, political virtues, a sense of right and liberty...spiritual riches...justice, friendship, happiness and virtue in the individual lives of all its members....They all constitute the good human life of the multitude.[40]

Jacques Maritain's application of Aquinas gave us a philosophy of hope, an encounter with God, and a corresponding call for each of us to use that encounter as our wellspring of energy to work for a better and more humane life for all. He wove philosophy, the works of St. Thomas Aquinas, and his Catholic faith into a reasoned call that our first duty is contemplative conversation with God, and our second is untiring work for the common good. Maritain said:

> [There, in the community of saints, the person no longer tends to emerge above the community....

> F]or it is in the church herself that its participation in the divine life is accomplished....For there is for the church a common work, which is continued redemption, to which each is ordained as the part of the work to the whole. But this common work is itself ordained to the personal good of each, to the union of each with God.[41]

Maritain provided another framework for understanding Jesus's call that "you shall love...your God with all your heart....You shall love your neighbor as yourself" (Mark 12:30–31).

By the time of his death, Jacques Maritain was perhaps the best-known Catholic philosopher in the world. Through his teaching positions in Paris and at Stanford University in the United States, his books, and his lectures, Maritain left a significant imprint on Catholic thought and secular society. Incredibly, someone who once considered suicide became one of the preeminent thinkers in the world.

> Finally, we turn to religious thought for the last word and find that the deepest layer of the human person's dignity consists in its property of resembling God....It is the image of God. For God is spirit and the human person proceeds from Him in having as principle of life a spiritual soul capable of knowing, loving and of being uplifted by grace to participate in the very life of God so that, in the end, it might know and love Him as He knows and loves himself.[42]

9. PRESIDENT JULIUS KAMBARAGE NYERERE

JULIUS KAMBARAGE NYERERE is considered "the father of the nation" by Tanzanians and was an international voice for a third way during the Cold War where nations were forced to choose between two opposing superpowers. His Catholic faith and commitment, however, is largely unknown outside Tanzania. He brought his faith into many arenas, as president of Tanganyika National Union (TANU), first president of Tanganyika, first president of the United Republic of Tanzania, and a leader in the Organization of African Unity.

Nyerere attempted to apply the Gospel to the pressing problems of real life: colonialism, underdevelopment, and uncompensated resource extraction. He, like many other leaders of newly freed nations, sought a path of national liberation without the exploitative features of U.S. capitalism or the rigidity of Soviet communism. President Nyerere sought to find a system that provided both economic stability and individual and collective freedom. As a result of his work, Nyerere is considered one of the leading East African leaders of the last century.

He began his public career not in politics but as a teacher in St. Mary's Catholic School in Tabora, Tanzania. He soon became active in the Makerere Debating Society. As was typical with such organizations, the debating society discussed critical social issues. Through analysis, study, and debate, Nyerere encountered the concept of African socialism. Essentially, some believed that the traditional African emphasis on communal decision-making could create a peaceful democratic socialist society.

Nyerere began to see politics as a venue both for national liberation and as a solution to poverty. Active in TANU, the party struggling for an end to colonialism, he was eventually selected as its president. When the United Republic of Tanzania was formed with the union of Tanganyika and Zanzibar, Nyerere was elected as its first president. Governing a large nation of one hundred different languages with a history of colonialism demanded vision and persistent faith.

To sustain and grow that faith, Julius Nyerere began each day at Mass. Nyerere said he attended daily Mass because he "believed that it is God who entrusted him with the responsibility to lead His people; therefore he had to begin each day with God's guidance and inspiration; he also had to ask for forgiveness for his service's imperfections."[43] Devoted to spreading the joy of the Gospel, Nyerere translated two catechisms and a hymnal into Zanaki, completed poetic translations of the Acts of the Apostles and the Gospels into Swahili, and studied papal encyclicals for spiritual guidance in the social world.

His belief in the dignity of humanity led to his emergence as a unique leader on the national stage. Unlike many African leaders who assumed power after liberation, Nyerere voluntarily stepped down from his office. While other leaders rigged elections, changed the constitution, or were deposed by coup, Nyerere served twenty-four years and then chose to step aside to allow a new generation of leaders to flourish.

During his time in office, Nyerere was well-known for his support of national liberation movements around the world, including South Africa, Palestine, Angola, and many others. In 1967, Nyerere released the Arusha Declaration, a call to action. The website Black Past recalls:

> This declaration emphasized self-reliance, frugality, and self-denial. It stated that everyone in the state, whatever his or her actual occupation, was a worker and that all means of production would be nationalized for the people. The concept of Ujamaa was the centerpiece of the social and economic development program. Here groups of village families worked together on communal farms for the common good. The Declaration also included a Leadership Code to promote equality among all Tanzania citizens. This code was one of numerous attempts to prevent party leaders and well-to-do individuals from forming privileged, exploitative groups. The Arusha Declaration as a whole sought to reduce the income inequality among all citizens and shift development efforts toward rural areas. It argued that the country was involved in a war against poverty and oppression.[44]

In addition to aiming for a self-sustaining economy, the Arusha Declaration reformed the education system. The three significant changes that it made were to emphasize primary education rather than secondary education, focus on practical knowledge over book knowledge, and promote education for agricultural skills. The Arusha Declaration is one of the most important political and economic decrees in Tanzania's history. It formally outlined how resources for development can be mobilized. All of these changes, motivated by the declaration, were aimed at creating a more self-reliant society. The application was more challenging than the promise, and collective farming and other components led to economic stagnation and decline. Though withdrawn after several years, the Declaration remains an example of human efforts to create a just society.

According to Nyerere, the former teacher, education was essential to creating a new society. In a 1976 speech titled "Adult Education and Development," Nyerere said:

> The primary function of Adult Education is to arouse a desire for change inspired by a conviction that there is a need for change; and that change is possible. People living in poverty, disease and exploitation are empowered to recognize that they too can move out of these miseries by their own actions, individually and in cooperation with others.…Therefore Adult Education is the vital source and force for developing a free people who are empowered to determine their own future.[45]

For over two decades, Nyerere tried to integrate Catholic social teaching on human development and African communal practices into the fabric of Tanzanian political life. There were some successes and many failed strategies. His vision of thriving self-sufficient, democratic communal societies was never realized. Yet, his leadership did improve income equality and increase adult literacy. He is also credited with building a unified nation, one that brought together 120 different tribes without chaotic civil wars and perpetual struggles for power. His legacy of peace, education, and equality are direct outcomes of his Catholic faith.

Much about his life reflects his Catholic faith. Friends and colleagues often described him as exuding charm, intelligence, and ethics that set him apart as a national leader. He was renowned for living simply among the people of Tanzania instead of in the presidential palace, avoiding corruption, driving his own small car around the nation, and spending his vacation working alongside villagers in the field. While the tradition had been to confer exalted titles upon leaders in Tanzania, he refused those designations and instead was known simply as Mwalimu, or "Teacher." A tireless servant in the cause of Tanzanian liberation, African progress, and human fulfillment, he once said, "I am simply a believer... in the world and human history. I believe in the equality and dignity of all human beings, and the duty to serve their well-being."[46]

Nyerere died on October 14, 1999, and Mwalimu was mourned by millions of Tanzanians. Years later, African economists, writers, scholars, and leaders held a conference in his honor. Some noted that one of his enduring legacies was providing the masses of Tanzanians—the poor, the marginalized, and the excluded—with "the language of possibility." His work to make society better for all was infused with this language of possibility; through education, cooperation, work, and prayer, humans as individuals and humans in community could create a better society. For Nyerere, this was the good news of the Gospel, in action among the people.

In a 1970 speech to the Maryknoll Sisters Conference, he noted:

> The church must work with the people in the positive tasks of building a future based on social justice. It must participate actively in initiating, securing, and creating, the changes which are necessary....Only by doing these things can the Church reduce hatred and promote its doctrine of love to all men.[47]

10. MARY LOU WILLIAMS

WERE THERE A GREATER sense of solidarity with Black Catholic spirituality by the larger Catholic community, the music of Mary Lou Williams would be incorporated into liturgy and Masses across the United States, and perhaps the world. Unknown perhaps to most Catholics, jazz innovator Mary Lou Williams was a devout Catholic. In addition to traditional jazz tunes, Mary Lou Williams composed hymns for her Catholic faith.

She was a true talent, and by age six she was known as the "little piano girl." When her family moved into a white neighborhood, they faced verbal insults which at times escalated into bricks thrown at their home. When the abuse stopped, her parents could not understand why. They later learned that the attackers were so mesmerized by Mary Lou's practice sessions that they called off their hateful acts to listen to her play the piano. In 1925, by age fifteen, Mary Lou Williams worked as a full-time musician.

Her musical career is vast in scope and versatility, for she was a virtuoso in ragtime, stride, swing, bop, blues, spirituals, gospel, and other forms of jazz. Duke Ellington called her "beyond category." She was both a talented pianist and one of the greatest composers and arrangers in the history of jazz. In the 1930s she was one of the masters of the Kansas City swing sound. The next decade, during the 1940s, Mary Lou Williams mentored Charlie Parker, Thelonious Monk, Dizzy Gillespie, and many others. Their collective impact on American creative music is a testament to the influence of Mary Lou Williams.

Like other jazz musicians in America, her greatness was little appreciated or properly compensated. Low-paying night clubs, exploitative record companies, and the availability of drugs and alcohol wreaked havoc on the jazz community. Though she never succumbed to the scourge of drugs, many of her fellow musicians did. Mary Lou watched helplessly as exploitation and addiction sapped creativity from her talented friends. Her dear friend, pianist Garland Wilson, died tragically in Paris. Following a 1954 performance in Paris, Mary Lou Williams noted that she felt overwhelmed with the evil and sadness all around her and walked off the stage with no intent to return. Withdrawing into seclusion, she searched the next three years for a spiritual center, a source of hope, and life's deeper meaning.

Returning to the United States, she looked to religion for answers, attending the famous Abyssinian Baptist Church in Harlem, a center of Black church activism under the leadership of Rev. Adam Clayton Powell Sr. Her quest led to visits to other churches in New York. Conversations with Barry Ulanov, a member of the Catholic intellectual group Thomas More Society, inspired her to explore some of the Catholic parishes in New York. Father Anthony S. Woods was moderator of the society, a parish priest, and a spiritual director who met with Mary Lou Williams for two years discussing faith and life.[48]

Encouraged by those conversations, Mary Lou Williams often dropped into Catholic churches to pray and meditate among the candles, statues, Stations of the Cross, and prayer chapels. In 1957 she joined the Roman Catholic Church, as did Dizzy Gillespie's wife Lorraine. Soon after her confirmation, Mary Lou opened her Harlem apartment to musicians struggling with addiction or depression. When other jazz musicians saw the positive impact of her work, many contributed funding to expand her outreach.

From 1962 to 1965, Pope John XXIII convened the Second Vatican Council, a global meeting that radically changed the direction of the entire church. One of the changes was a more active participation of the laity in the sacred liturgy as well as increased use of vernacular language and forms of creative worship. Mary Lou Williams, composer and arranger extraordinaire, determined to express her faith through the power and creativity of jazz. Upon becoming Catholic, she learned of St. Martin de Porres, an Afro-Peruvian saint who was recognized for his service to the poor, hungry, and sick of Peru. She sought to highlight his devotion to God and the poor through music, and she composed a tribute to de Porres, the first Black canonized saint. Williams studied his life and work and spent weeks in her Harlem apartment on a composition in his honor. *Black Christ of the Andes* debuted on his feast day, November 3, 1963, at St. Francis Xavier parish in New York City. She considered St. Martin de Porres, through his selfless dedication to Peru's poor, Indigenous, and Black population, as a "Christ" to the lost. In the great tradition of the community of saints, she also calls on de Porres, the "Black Christ of the Andes," to intervene for our salvation.

Proud of her Catholic faith and Black heritage, Mary Lou Williams sought to place St. Martin de Porres within the pantheon of Catholic saints with the likes of St. Clare of Assisi and St. Francis who selflessly served God and others. *Black Christ of the Andes* also had political implications, for her composition appeared during the height of the civil rights struggle, before the Black Power movement. By placing "Black" in front of "Christ," her music and message predated James Cone's groundbreaking *Black Theology and Black Power.* She lifted Blackness from the derogatory and negative to the divine and beloved. Through music, Mary Lou Williams emphasized her race and faith so the world could see the gift of both. Furthermore, she saw jazz as a creative way to call forth the Spirit as we honor our saints and look to be inspired in our respective spiritual journeys. Following the example of St. Martin de Porres, her music was intended to heal ailing souls.[49]

Once during a visit to Rome, she met with Monsignor Joseph Gremillion, secretary of the Pontifical Commission on Justice and Peace. Their conversation inspired her to write a *Mass for Peace.* Through this work she wanted to express hope during the Vietnam War, racial violence, and poverty. Elements of jazz, gospel, and the blues infused the *Mass for Peace* with a contemporary message. The composition was first performed at Holy Family Church, on East 47th Street in New York, and was in honor of assassinated Kenyan president Tom Mboya.

In 1971 famed choreographer Alvin Ailey wanted to build a dance around the score of *Mass for Peace.* Ailey and Williams collaborated on what was titled *Mary Lou's Mass.* The two also included tributes to Rev. Dr. Martin Luther King Jr., such as pieces titled, *I Have a Dream* and *Tell Them Not to Talk Too Long.* Other compositions—*People in Trouble, Jesus Is the Best,* and *Lazarus*—speak directly to Black struggle, religious faith, and ultimate redemption. The dance and music production combined Catholic liturgical prayers, Black Baptist social activism, jazz, and creative dance.

Mary Lou Williams later taught jazz in Pittsburgh's Catholic high schools and at Duke University. She promoted music both as an art form and a source of healing. Once she worked with artist David Stone Martin to develop a roots and branches visual on the origins and evolution of music. The tree diagram included branches like the spirituals, ragtime, blues, jazz, gospel, and other music. Williams placed "suffering" as the root and foundation of all the branches.[50] From her experience, Williams saw suffering as the basis of creative music. Further, since music was born in grief, it can speak directly to suffering and transform that pain into joy and hope.

By the time of her death on May 28, 1981, Mary Lou Williams had left significant musical imprints on jazz, Catholic spirituality, and Black faith.

> What I am trying to do is bring back good jazz to you with the healing in it and the spiritual feeling.…It's all spiritual music and healing to the soul.[51]

PART III

PRIESTS

Priests will be helped…by cultivating those qualities which are rightly held in high esteem in human relations, qualities such as goodness of heart, sincerity, strength, and constancy of mind, careful attention to justice, courtesy, and others.

Decree on the Ministry and Life of Priests,
Presbyterorum Ordinis (3)

1. FATHER PEDRO ARRUPE, SJ

FATHER PEDRO ARRUPE was superior general of the Society of Jesus (Jesuit Order) until a devastating stroke left him partially paralyzed and severely compromised his ability to speak. In 1983, his final address to the Society at the Thirty-Third General Congregation had to be read by Father Ignacio Iglesias. A portion of that speech is now included in prayer books and on prayer cards:

> More than ever I find myself in the hands of God. This is what I have wanted all my life, from my youth. And this is still the one thing I want. But now there is a difference: the initiative is entirely with God. It is indeed a profound spiritual experience to know and feel myself entirely in his hands.[1]

This expression of faith in the midst of tragedy and limitation continues to inspire.

Father Arrupe was ordained a Jesuit priest in 1936. Twenty-nine years later, in 1965, he was elected as superior general of the Society of Jesus. He served in that role for seventeen years until his retirement in 1983. Despite forty-seven years as a priest and leader in the Catholic Church, it was at the end of his ministry, in the middle of debilitating pain and loss, that he exclaimed he had achieved his desire: to be entirely in the hands of God.

His final address emphatically asserts that "the initiative is entirely with God." This humble statement declares that while much is made of our own power to decide—to repent, convert, and act—it is God who is in control. Father Arrupe echoes the words of Jesus in John's Gospel: "You have not chosen me but I have chosen you" (John 15:16). The superior general learned from suffering what he had struggled to attain his entire life. Arrupe recognized that God makes the first and definitive move toward us; in creation, the incarnation, the gift of the Holy Spirit, God surrounds and embraces us.

This insight is not the only contribution of Father Pedro Arrupe. His first missionary assignment as a Jesuit was to Japan, with full duties contingent upon him learning the Japanese language. When the United States declared war on Japan after the Pearl Harbor attack, Father Arrupe was arrested on charges of espionage and held in solitary confinement. He was released in 1942 after suffering treatment he described as "excruciating."

After release from prison, the Jesuits sent him to Nagatsuka to become the master of novices. Nagatsuka was just outside of Hiroshima. On August 6, 1945, on the Feast of the Transfiguration, the day revealing Christ's dazzling glory, Hiroshima was incinerated by an atomic bomb. Arrupe was in the novitiate building during the blast and saw the blinding flash as seismic waves threw him to the floor and showered him with glass, plaster, and debris. In later years, Arrupe spoke against the use of atomic weapons and described the streams of bleeding, burned, and tattered bodies stumbling along the road from Hiroshima. Arrupe estimated that 150,000 people came through his city in desperate search for help. Prior to the priesthood, he had begun studies in medicine, so he drew on that training to establish a makeshift hospital at the novitiate. He and his fellow priests took in 150 of the straggling wounded and treated them with whatever resources they could gather.

Later, he and his colleagues entered Hiroshima where

he witnessed horrors. An entire city was in ruins, burned and wounded people begged for help, children with glass and splinters embedded in their bodies stumbled about, disfigured children called for parents, and frantic parents screamed for their children. Arrupe said the tragedies worsened at nightfall, as the wounded who sought comfort in the river water laid by the riverbank. When the tide rose, they became stuck in the mud, too burned or tired to move, their drowning cries for help filling the air. He also describes people with burned bodies in places where there was no fire and others frantically trying to save trapped family members. Statistics cannot convey the tragedy; some estimate fifty thousand people died in the blast and another one hundred thousand died later from burns, radiation, and injuries.

The Hiroshima explosion and its aftermath radically changed Father Arrupe's life. The mass horror grounded his faith in God and revealed the power of humanity to destroy life. He also used the image of atomic energy to call for a return to God. He wrote:

> When will humanity...glimpse...a new reality encased in all being: the divine reality? Above all, when will we discover that in the core of our person there lives that divine reality? For this we will need a flash of light far more powerful than that which blinded us at Hiroshima: the light of faith which illuminates without blinding because it is both powerful and gentle. On that day, when humans discover, through the light of faith, God—in themselves and in their fellow humans—and see that this God...is a God of love, war and violence will cease and hatred will be no more. God will be...the cause of true union. On that day

> will be born a new humanity, that of the children of God.[2]

Father Arrupe was elected superior general of the Jesuit Order in 1965, the same year Vatican II ended. These were pivotal years both in the global Catholic Church and in the Jesuit Order, and some consider his leadership as a "re-founding" of the Society of Jesus. Feeding off of the energy of Vatican II, Arrupe emphasized collegiality, solidarity with the poor, and discernment and prayer as hallmarks of Jesuit life. Many described him as a "man of prayer engaging the world" as he confronted issues of injustice, war, and poverty.

In 1973 he called together the Thirty-Second General Congregation of the Order for further reflection on the teachings of Vatican II. As the world faced the Cold War, anticolonial struggles, and the emergence of movements for liberation, the Jesuits responded with radical calls for justice and mercy. During the meeting, Arrupe declared, "What is it to be a companion of Jesus today? It is to engage, under the standard of the Cross, in the crucial struggle of our time, the struggle for faith and that struggle for justice which it includes."[3] The Congregation also emphasized the theme, "faith that does justice," a defining hallmark of the Jesuit order even today.

It can be said that the legacy of Fr. Pedro Arrupe began with his first vows as a Jesuit, was seared into his soul in Hiroshima, and flourished in his implementation of the teachings of Vatican II. He embodied Catholic emphasis on the dignity of the human person and the role of the Christian alongside humanity on the road to a loving human community.

Father Arrupe's faith and practice was grounded in devotion to the Sacred Heart of Christ. On several occasions he urged the Society of Jesus to rekindle devotion to the

Sacred Heart of Christ. He believed God's immense love, as expressed in the Sacred Heart, would inspire us all to greater acts of mercy and justice. He once wrote:

> Heart of Jesus. All the love of Christ, God and man, sent by the Father through the Spirit, who offers himself in redemption for all, and with each of us establishes a personal relationship....Christ in his incarnation intervenes in the established relationship of man with God and completely transforms it. The great power which effects this revolution, the great novelty of the New Alliance is the love of his heart, and the love he comes to kindle in each one of us.[4]

2. FATHER DANIEL BERRIGAN, SJ

DANIEL BERRIGAN, ALONG with his brother Philip, was synonymous for decades with nonviolent protest, pacifism, and peace and justice movements. Berrigan's life of prophetic activism began in the 1960s and did not end until his death in 2016. Father Berrigan emerged in the 1960s as a leader in the Roman Catholic "new left," exposing racism, militarism, and capitalist greed as contributors to an unjust and dehumanizing society. Philip Berrigan was a Josephite priest from 1955 to 1973 and a courageous participant in struggles for peace.

"The Berrigan brothers" burned draft cards, were arrested at nuclear weapons facilities, and visited Vietnam. For burning draft cards in Catonsville, Maryland, they were arrested and sentenced to prison. Like Dr. Martin Luther King Jr., arrest and jail were common features of their ministry. Daniel and Philip Berrigan were arrested again when Plowshares activists, who worked to end weapons of war and mass destruction, protested the General Electric missile plant, and again for blocking the entrance to the naval museum in Manhattan. The Berrigan brothers cofounded the Catholic Peace Fellowship, maintained friendships with Dorothy Day and Thomas Merton, and in 1968 traveled to Hanoi with Howard Zinn to see the horrors of war and to rescue three U.S. soldiers.

Daniel Berrigan's protests against the madness of nuclear weapons and the horror of war grew out of his Catholic conviction of the dignity of humans and the presence of God in all of life and creation. Some also believe

Philip and Daniel's opposition to violence had its origins in years of experiencing their father's abuse of their mother. While some who witness or experience domestic violence later become perpetrators, Philip and Daniel were impelled toward a lifetime of antiviolent activism.

Daniel Berrigan's perspective on the Catholic call to peace and engagement also formed during his assignment to France shortly after his ordination. He was influenced by the French "worker-priests" of the late 1940s and 1950s. These priests lived and worked alongside oppressed workers and understood that the good news of Christ must speak to their concerns for basic dignity and security. The worker-priests gave him a model and vision of what the church should be in our world.

As a teacher of theology, a poet, and a writer, Daniel Berrigan infused his lectures and writings with calls for peace and justice. One of his books, *The Nightmare of God: The Book of Revelation*, reveals his uncompromising stand for peace, the end of war, and the dismantling of all nuclear weapons. Berrigan tells us that the Book of Revelation exposes the discord and violence that fuels the ugly reality of history's downward spiral. He reminds us that the misery around us comes from human acts, not the work of God. Berrigan tells us that interactions between and within families, races, political parties, and nations are marred by discord, self-absorption, and domination. These are not the ways of God. In linking "Babylon" with the empires of the world, he writes:

> Each successive empire seizes on the ancient crimes, dusts them off, justifies them anew.... Under this weight we lie prone, sunken to the ground, our imaginations chilled with death, our "way of life" revealed for the way of death it is, our crimes turning us by day into zombies, and

> by night into vessels churning with nightmare.... It is hard to remind ourselves of such realities. "On to the next horror, think the people"..."On to the next military adventure" exult the generals.... Babylon's moral life is not a passage from crime to repentance, but only from crime to crime....From no one we hear, "remember and repent," only, "forget and forget." Thus our history becomes a progressive breakaway from all restraint.[5]

The picture painted by Father Berrigan is confirmed when we recount our own nation's history. He says we are a nation who has bent the knee to the idols of money, ego, machines of war, competition, nuclear weapons, and violence; we have succumbed to the power of death. Founded on the extermination of Indigenous people and the sale, torture, rape, and murder of Africans transported against their will, the nation staggers under its founding realities. Unjustified war against Mexico and the theft of half their nation, lynchings and massacres of Black citizens, the adoration of guns regardless of the human cost, the absence of social safety nets and health care—our nation resembles Revelation's Babylon.

Father Berrigan does offer Christians and people of good will a path forward. An oft-forgotten passage in the book of Revelation must serve as our response to the violence and death of empire. Berrigan cites Revelation as his, and our, calling: "He placed his right hand on me, saying, Do not be afraid; I am the first and the last, and the living one. I was dead, and see, I am alive for ever and ever" (Rev 1:18). Berrigan believed Jesus was alive, and as the bringer of the good news of God's reign, his living presence compels us to move forward. He writes that since Jesus lives now, tomorrow, and forever, we are liberated from "one-night stands of conscience" to a lifetime commitment to work for life against death, peace against violence, and mercy against revenge.

Berrigan reminds us that until Jesus comes again to fulfill God's ultimate liberation, the "meantime" of now is most important. The future of a gathered humanity and our eternal life in the light of God inspires us to create in part what we will know in full. Berrigan says we read Revelation and look at our current troubles and forget that Christ, who was once dead, tells us, "See, I am alive for ever and ever." Christ is alive, and the good news of great joy that accompanied his birth is made real by our faithfulness despite the powers arrayed against us. Daniel Berrigan and his brother Philip lived their lives as testament that Christ is no longer dead but is alive, for ever and forever.

On his eightieth birthday, Berrigan said, "On the day after I'm embalmed, that's the day I will give up."[6] Those who saw his life unfold were not surprised by this pronouncement. He worked and spoke for justice everywhere he went, angering many along the way. Some of America's Jewish community accused him of anti-Semitism when he supported the Palestinian people's desire for self-determination and an end to Israeli settlements and repression. His opposition to America's wars, from Vietnam to Grenada to Iraq to Afghanistan, led governments, many Catholic bishops, and even the Vatican to consider him unpatriotic. In his later years, he assisted AIDS victims in New York and participated in the Occupy movement in 2016.

For Berrigan, his brother Philip, and many others engaged in the movements for peace and justice, opposition was not a reason to give up but rather proof that they had touched the nerve center of an antihuman "Babylon." And unlike Babylon, which in the Book of Revelation falls under the weight of its own violence and thirst for power and domination, the Jesus Berrigan follows is "alive for ever and ever."

Many considered Daniel and Philip Berrigan "heretics," "troublemakers," "traitors," "anti-Semitics," but others looked to them as models of the risen Christ. Their commitment to peace was not founded on others' opinions, prevailing views, or the status quo. It was a fundamental element of being Catholic, being Christian, and being human.

3. FATHER IGNACIO ELLACURÍA, SJ

INCREDIBLY, FEW IN THE United States acknowledge the nation's role in past crimes committed against the peasants of El Salvador and Nicaragua. In the 1980s, under Democratic and Republican presidential administrations, the U.S. government provided financial and military support to forces that murdered civilians in Central America. Among those murdered were priests, nuns, laypeople, and theologians whose crime was solidarity with the poor and commitment to a just economy.

During the night of November 16, 1989, an elite battalion of U.S.-trained El Salvadoran military surrounded the Central American University with the "orders to kill Fr. Ignacio Ellacuría and leave no witnesses."[7] Father Ellacuría was the president of the university, and his prophetic homilies, writings, and negotiations for peace endangered the unjust status quo. The soldiers executed six members of the Jesuit community—Ignacio Ellacuría, Ignacio Martín-Baro, Segundo Montes, Juan Ramón Moreno, Joaquín López y López, and Amando López—and their housekeeper, Elba Ramos, and the housekeeper's sixteen-year-old daughter Célina Ramos. These eight threats to national security were forced to lie down in the courtyard and were then shot in the head at close range with heavy automatic weapons. Outside of a few Jesuit universities and some Catholic and progressive circles, this slaughter has little recognition.

Ellacuría's path from priest to martyr is a most unlikely one. In his early years of study, he was a devotee of Spanish philosopher Xavier Zubiri, a major voice in Spain, whose contribution to philosophy was his "religation theory" of reality.[8] He surmised that an individual's self-awareness and their understanding and connection to God was grounded in the individual's fulfillment of the tasks and duties they are obliged to complete in the context of their family, society, and nation. From 1940 to 1980, Zubiri deeply influenced Spanish philosophy.

Ellacuría also studied with Karl Rahner, the influential Jesuit theologian. Rahner taught that theology was the science of faith, our conscious explanation of God's revelation to us. Ellacuría also learned from Rahner that theology must be rooted in history and reality. Therefore, concepts like the reign of God, salvation, and grace are only understood as concrete historical realities.

Grounded in these teachings, Ignacio Ellacuría was assigned to El Salvador where his theology collided with the scandal of economic and social inequality, poverty, and violence. While traditional Catholic teachings encouraged a fatalistic acceptance of suffering, Ellacuría's theology thrust upon him the obligation of cocreating God's reign of justice and mercy in the midst of suffering.

By his own testimony, the other catalyst that thrust Ellacuría into the crucible of El Salvadoran politics was the 1980 murder of Archbishop Oscar Romero. The archbishop was a powerful voice against the poverty of the masses and the elite's use of power to enforce their suffering. His homilies, radio broadcasts, and calls for peace were silenced when an assassin murdered him in a small chapel as he was saying Mass.

As president of the Central American University in San Salvador, Ellacuría transformed the school into a center for Christian solidarity with the poor. The university hosted classes and seminars to empower common people in their liberation from oppression. The university's students learned from Zubiri and Rahner that our relation to God is found in our duty to humanity, and that salvation is meaningless without observable realities.

Like Romero, Ellacuría condemned the government's war on the peasants. In the civil war between the government and leftist insurgents, Ellacuría promoted dialogue and negotiations. He and others in El Salvador pleaded with the leftists, the government, the elite, and the moderate and center voices to join a dialogue to end violence and work for a just society. They demanded education, employment, and justice for the poor. This work put Ellacuría and the Jesuits of the Central American University on a deadly collision course with the El Salvadoran rich, the military, and their U.S. backers.

While on retreat with Ignatius of Loyola's Spiritual Exercises, Ellacuría confronted his own calling. Week One of the Exercises asks the retreatant "to kneel before the Cross of Jesus and ask, 'What have I done for Christ? What am I doing for Christ? What ought I do for Christ?'" Ellacuría adapted the colloquy, or conversation before the cross, to ask, in light of the suffering masses, "upon the people thus crucified…what have I done to crucify them? What am I doing to uncrucify them? What ought I do so that this people will be raised?"[9] This conversation before Jesus on the cross further strengthened him to commit his life for the complete liberation of the poor. Ellacuría, his fellow Jesuits, and the poor and peasants they worked among believed that "history," the realm of real life inhabited by real people, was the only place the freedom, justice, and love of God's reign could be realized. Otherwise, God, God's reign, and the Gospel, are irrelevant illusions.

I once was in an online meeting with a Jesuit priest who attended a memorial for Ellacuría and the other seven martyrs at the Central American University in San Salvador. The priest noted at the time of the event that his spiritual life was stale and his vocation empty. While attending the memorial, he was struck by the rose garden planted by the husband of martyred housekeeper Elba Ramos. When the visiting priest saw roses bloom amid death, he was reminded that resurrection after crucifixion is real, and we should never lose heart.

Ellacuría's last major essay before his murder was "Utopia and Propheticism from Latin America: A Concrete Essay in Historical Soteriology." There he argued Christ creates in us "a new human being," where Christ is "reproduced" in our lives. He wrote:

> This new human being is defined in part by active protest and permanent struggle. This new human being seeks to overcome the dominant cultural injustice that is considered an evil…because it keeps most of the human population in conditions of inhumane living.…The motive of this new human being who is moved by the Spirit is not hatred but mercy and love, for all are seen as children of God and not as enemies to be destroyed.… Along with love comes hope. To be really new, the new human beings must be persons of hope and of joy in the building of a more just world.[10]

Ellacuría and his colleagues were aware of the risks of their commitment. They knew many priests and laypeople, and even the archbishop, who had been assassinated. Ellacuría himself often wrote that the reign of God must of necessity be in conflict with a history and reality configured by the power of sin. In the essay "On Liberation," he wrote:

> It is in receiving the spirit of Christ and being moved by it that the Church may contribute to lib-

eration, creatively doing today what Jesus did, in his own time, and, as best it can, to do so as Jesus did, preferentially from the poor, for the poor, and as the poor. If the church fills its life with the Spirit of Christ and cultivates its prophetic potential, it can, from the gospel itself,...be a radical force for liberation.[11]

4. FATHER RUTILIO GRANDE, SJ

THE DEATH OF FR. RUTILIO Grande transformed Archbishop Oscar Romero into a prophet of liberation for the poor. Father Grande was murdered in a hail of bullets outside a village in El Salvador.

The book *When the Gospel Grows Feet* by Thomas Kelly describes the path that led to Grande's assassination. Rutilio Grande was born on July 5, 1928, in the El Salvadoran village of El Paisnal. His parents separated when he was a child, and he was raised by his grandmother and older brother. He followed the path of his devout grandmother, and while other children were outside playing, Rutilio set up altars in the house and "played" church. His faith grew with age, and at thirteen Grande enrolled in seminary. He later took Jesuit novitiate vows, and in 1959 was ordained a priest in the Society of Jesus.

Rutilio Grande struggled with mental health challenges, and in addition to depression, he suffered two nervous breakdowns during his priestly formation. Despite those setbacks and obstacles, Grande continued in his vocation as a priest.

Thomas Kelly sets Grande's life in the context of changes within the Catholic Church during those years. He notes three pivotal events in the church. The first is Vatican II, asking the church to experience the "joys and hopes" of the world and that the "people of God" embrace service to humanity. The second was Pope Paul VI's encyclical *Populo-*

rum Progressio, calling the church to be engaged in the integral development of every human person.

The third event was the Latin American Bishops conference held in Medellín in 1968. The conference, often referred to as Medellín, was titled "The Church in the Present-day Transformation of Latin America in the Light of the Council" [Vatican II]. The bishops affirmed, "it appears to be a time full of zeal for full emancipation, of liberation from every form of servitude, of personal maturity and collective integration."[12] In expressing solidarity with the majority poor of the continent, "we wish to feel the problems…share the agonies…and cooperate in the solutions."[13] All three events provided Grande with the blueprint for his concrete activity among the poor of El Salvador.

One of his first assignments was teaching in the Jesuit seminary in El Salvador, and during his time there he often visited his hometown of El Paisnal. In his interactions with the local people, Grande became increasingly aware of the deadly effects of poverty, the vast inequality of rich and poor, and the violent response of the government and those with power to calls for justice. His conversations with the poor resonated with what he learned through Vatican II, *Populorum Progressio,* and Medellín.

After teaching, Father Grande served as a priest in El Salvador. In his early days as a pastor, he sought to blend traditional peasant piety with concrete acts on behalf of the poor. While this work yielded some benefits, social action in this life was often undermined by overemphasis on the life to come in heaven. As Grande sought to find a way to bring the promises of new life to the people, his life was transformed during a three-month program at the Pastoral Institute for Latin America (IPLA) in Quito, Ecuador, in 1972. Bishop Leonidas

Proaño led the IPLA for ordained and laypeople to enhance their ministry through theological reflection and discussion.

Grande returned from the institute with renewed vigor. He was assigned to the town of Aguilares and soon developed what he called "The Grand Missionary Tour."

Not the "missionary" approach of "we've come to save you," this disciplined program walked alongside and empowered the poor for their own development. Grande and his supporters listened to the townspeople, learned their issues, and helped uncover their own gifts and strengths. The community then held meetings to develop a common vision of the most important challenges, followed by a discussion of potential remedies. Grande and his colleagues then helped the community determine who among them would play leadership roles, and those selected leaders were provided training and skill building for servant-leadership. Becoming a leader was a serious duty, because leaders were asked to commit time and resources to the community. Finally, from among those leaders, the community selected a few called Delegates of the Word. These received more training, particularly to learn the practical aspects of a "new understanding of the gospel, and of the kingdom of God." The delegates were confirmed before the whole community on Pentecost Sunday, publicly proclaiming:

> Our only politics are to be faithful proclaimers of the Gospel which has to do with all human activities aligned with God in order to transform the world. We will denounce with energy and without pretense, all sorts of injustice and abuse against the human person, wherever they come from.... Our goal is to build together with you, a community of brothers and sisters, committed to build

> a new world without oppressors and oppressed, according to the plan of God.[14]

Thus commissioned, Delegates of the Word became advocates for the whole community, and were involved in agriculture cooperatives, civic education, and strikes led by the Christian Federation of El Salvadoran Peasants (FECCAS). Father Grande established thirty-seven base communities and trained 326 leaders, including 231 Delegates of the Word, each of whom engaged in various forms of community empowerment. As the work of Father Grande and the Grand Missionary Tour gained popularity and tangible benefits for the poor, the government, the military, and the elite of El Salvador took notice. They saw the Delegates of the Word and Father Grande as threats to the established order. El Salvador was a stratified society, where 81 percent of the arable land was owned by a dozen families. Furthermore, the El Salvadoran government was backed by the United States, whose Cold War blinders saw every movement for the poor as communist subversion. Therefore, the government and right-wing militias of El Salvador believed they defended a righteous cause in their use of violence against movements for justice.

Father Grande continued to urge the Grand Missionary Tour forward, and in one of his last homilies he noted:

> Many people prefer a Christ of undertakers and morticians. They want a mute Christ, without a mouth, who passed by them walking in the streets. Many prefer Christ with a muzzle on his mouth. Many prefer a Christ made for our own whims and according to our own interests. This is not the Christ of the Gospels…who gave his life for the noblest cause of humanity.[15]

Shortly after that homily, on March 12, 1977, Father Grande was murdered while driving through El Paisnal. Gunmen in a pickup truck pulled up behind him while other shooters positioned on both sides of a creek channel opened fire. Father Grande, seventy-two-year-old Manuel Solórzano, and fifteen-year-old Nelson Lemur were killed that day. The three "subversives" were on their way to celebrate a novena in honor of that town's feast day.

Hundreds of people walked miles to attend his memorial Mass, and the celebration of his life lasted until midnight. As the bodies were interned in the floor of the church, someone proclaimed, "Rutilio's walk with El Paisnal is like Christ's journey with the cross."[16] That journey, like Christ's, did not end in death, for Bishop Romero and many others followed, and continue to follow, the path of Fr. Rutilio Grande.

5. FATHER BERNARD HÄRING, CSSR

BERNARD HÄRING'S JOURNEY began with an idyllic life in a German village, continued on the Eastern Front during World War II, and flourished as he became the foremost Catholic moral theologian of his time. He was born into a Catholic family in a serene Bavarian village and confirmed when he was eight years old. Afterward he spoke excitedly about his experience of a vision of Jesus Christ. He told his sister Konstantine, "I think I want to be a saint." Like a good older sibling, she resisted sarcasm and replied, "Well, why not?"[17]

Bernard felt the call to be a priest, and he joined the Redemptorist Order, being ordained in 1939, the year the second deadly global war began. Father Häring was drafted into the German army and assigned duties as both a chaplain and a medic. His autobiography, *Free and Faithful*, describes the chilling details of his war duty. Committed to the mercy and faithfulness of the Catholic faith, he lived his calling in the most unlikely of places. While in France he aided both French and German wounded and said Mass, against Nazi policies, for German soldiers and French civilians. On the Western front he led Bible classes for captured Protestant soldiers and in the East baptized the children of Eastern Orthodox families in villages where the priests were absent. Within the brutality of the Russian front, he provided care for Russian soldiers and peasants, along with the German wounded. Once when his regiment was surrounded by Russian soldiers, peasants under his care showed him an escape route. In Russia and Poland, he warned Jews when the SS would be arriving and helped them escape. Not every German was a hardened Nazi, and Häring gave last rites to many sorrowful, repentant young German soldiers. Häring later described his war experience as the definitive transformation of his ministry and life. He experienced the consequences of blind obedience, the senselessness of war, and the horrors suffered by all, including the innocent, the children, and the helpless.

After the war, Häring was assigned by the Redemptorists to study moral theology. He was disappointed with that assignment, for he viewed moral theology as abstract and irrelevant. Upon embarking on his studies, however, he transformed moral theology from lifeless dogma into a source of life-giving insights.

Häring wrote the influential multivolume *The Law of Christ: Moral Theology for Priests and Laity.* This project opened moral theology from a subject primarily for priests to a concern for all Catholics. The dust jacket of volume 1 notes, "The theme…of the Law of Christ is that the moral life properly consists, not simply in the fulfillment of a series of impersonal principles, but in an affirmative response to the call from Christ, an imitation of Him…as a member of His Body, animated by His Spirit."[18]

The war left an indelible imprint on Häring regarding the consequences of blind obedience. He saw the devastation resulting from Germany's capitulation to Nazism and Hitler. Häring himself was brutally interrogated by German soldiers who later said they were just "following orders." Therefore, in his reflections on moral theology, Häring saw that responsibility must replace obedience as an operative feature in a life of faith. Thus, a significant theme in *The Law of Christ* is not obedience to church hierarchy and tradition but responsibility to God and all humanity. He writes:

> Religion truly lived must have as essential characteristic the element of response. Response, responsibility and dialogue belong to religion essentially. We have religion only if man conceives of the Holy as a Power that advances toward him and to whom we respond in dialogue.[19]

As we respond to God's loving advance toward us, we then act responsibly toward God and others.

In *The Law of Christ,* Häring wrote, "Religion…comprises two essential themes, God in the glory of His love, and man in the favor of God's grace. True community of persons is possible only if two persons commune seriously."[20] For Häring, moral theology is grounded in our ongoing dialogue with a loving God. Our encounter with God does not lead to isolated piety but opens us to all humanity. "Religion as community with God is also the foundation of the human community, the genuine fellowship of persons."[21]

Fr. Bernard Häring was among the Catholic theologians whose insights influenced the documents of Vatican II. Häring was a key contributor to the two Constitutions on the role of the church, *Lumen Gentium* and *Gaudium et Spes.* His experience in war solidified his commitment to peace, and he was instrumental in *Gaudium et Spes* section 5 on fostering peace in the world. Häring said, "I consider my work on *Gaudium et Spes* one of the high points of my life."[22]

Häring contributed to Catholic theology and practice in other ways. He promoted Catholic openness to diverse cultures and the recognition that God's grace is operative among all humanity and is not dependent on the arrival of European missionaries. On trips to Africa, Asia, and Latin

America, he recognized the inherent dignity of the peoples of those regions as well as the value of their religious life.

Häring also worked with religious orders to enhance their prayer life both for personal growth and social action. Inspired by the prophet Isaiah's words, "these I will bring to my holy mountain, and make them joyful in my house of prayer" (56:7), Häring proposed that religious orders dedicate one building to a "house of prayer." This practice is credited with a renewal of both prayer and service in many religious communities.

Father Häring lived the theme of responsibility over obedience. In opposition to the church hierarchy, he supported women's ordination and was critical of the church's rigid stance on birth control.

Häring responded to God's grace with dialogue with God and love for humanity. Though many of his positions generated controversy from the Vatican, he remained free and faithful, free to respond to the God of grace, and faithful to his call as a channel for the good news.

> Christian moral theology...must remain true to this basic model. Those who preach salvation, those who attend to salvation by caring for others, and those to whom they speak must have an immediate sense that God sets us free for true life by the powerful gift of his love and grace. More than anything else, we want to be servants of joy. Then it will be evident that joy in God is our greatest source of strength.[23]

6. FATHER HANS KÜNG

FATHER HANS KÜNG is one of the many priests, religious, and theologians who at one time or another were investigated by the Vatican's Congregation for the Doctrine of the Faith. Like his colleagues, Küng simultaneously loved the church and publicly disagreed with positions he believed were inconsistent with the God of love and life. From his idyllic Swiss childhood to becoming a priest, professor of theology, theologian at Vatican II, and critic of Catholic teaching and practice, Hans Küng is arguably one of the most influential Catholics of the last one hundred years.

Küng's writings and teachings are rooted in the mystery of God; the life, passion, and resurrection of Jesus Christ; and the reality of the Holy Spirit. For Küng, some of God's immensity is contained in the Catholic Church, and some, if not most, is beyond it. Küng is loyal to the Catholic Church to the extent it reflects his understanding of God. Where the church does not, he, out of love for the church, seeks to open it more to the movement of the Holy Spirit. His critiques are motivated by love for God and love for the church.

Hans Küng believed that what troubled the church were not his criticisms but rather unexamined traditions contrary to God's desire for a people journeying to be "one." He questioned church teaching on women's leadership and ordination, (*Women in Christianity*), the authority of the Pope (*Infallible?*), church hierarchy (*The Council, Reform and Reunion*), and rigidity, exclusion, and self-righteousness (*Can We Save the Catholic Church?*). He also questioned mandatory celibacy and church teaching on LGTBQ people, noting that the church often covers ill-founded human practice with the veneer of divine inspiration. Once the label of "God-ordained" attaches to a tradition, it seems immune to modification or even discussion.

Freedom, for Küng, is the goal and purpose of human life. His understanding of freedom was not an unfettered individualism but rather the freedom to be open to the Spirit of God. His first memoir, *My Struggle for Freedom*, is a testimony to his perspective that we can only respond to God if we are free. Therefore, stifling structures, capitulation to societal norms, and obsession with self are all obstacles to our ability to respond to the freedom of God.

On his eventful 1963 trip to the United States, he records a university colleague's comments on his insistent talk of freedom by noting, "I know that there is the Church; I know that there is freedom, but I didn't know that the church and freedom go together."[24] Later, during an address at Yale University Divinity School, Küng describes freedom as a gift and a task. He notes that freedom should be the basic structure and inner being of the church, and that we should constantly be aware of the tendency to confuse our own ideology with God's revelation. For Küng, "it is tragic that particularly in modern times countless people have fled from the church, the original sphere of freedom, to seek freedom in the world."[25]

His memoir includes a chapter titled "Abiding Insights" on the important role of Ignatius of Loyola's Spiritual Exercises in his life. Küng writes that he maintained a journal where he often asked himself, "What am I living for?" He answers:

> *Ad maiorem Dei gloriam* "to the greater glory of God": time and again I keep writing AMDG in my diary over the beginning of the year. This is

> to remind me of the meaning of human life; not living for myself but for my creator and perfector, origin and goal: God alone as the absolute, everything else on earth relative. To live to God's glory and not simply for myself.[26]

Among many other activities, Küng is known for his work for peace in the world through the collaboration and full engagement of all the world's religions. He was president of the Global Ethic Foundation, an organization that promotes the idea that all religions share foundational ethics that, if practiced, could overcome divisions regarding secondary beliefs. Further, he drafted the Global Ethic Declaration of the Parliament of World Religions in 1993. Küng met with global leaders to promote the vision of world peace, an urgent necessity given that funds expended on war making could be transferred to benefit human health and well-being. He met with General Secretary of the Communist Party of the Soviet Union Mikhail Gorbachev, United Nations Secretary-General Kofi Annan, and many others to discuss making peace a reality in our world.

His book *The Church Maintained in Truth: A Theological Meditation* prompted an investigation and eventual censure by the Congregation for the Defense of the Faith (CDF). In his 1979 publication, Küng argues that allegiance to Jesus Christ is the foundation and norm for truth and that no pope, bishop, or institution has sole access to or authority over God's truth. He wrote that truth is not fixed but is an ever-greater reality uncovered during our collective journey as the People of God. He also notes that because God and truth are without limits, the church could at times be in error. Küng says this is borne out because past teachings, papal doctrines, and former ecumenical councils were sometimes in error and have since been revisited. Küng maintained that errors are part of our journey toward God's truth. He wrote, "If sin could become a "happy fault" (*felix culpa*)...might not error...become a 'happy error' (*felix error*) since the truth of the gospel shines out all the more brightly through the Church's errors?"[27] Thus, rather than fear dialogue, Hans Küng encourages us to boldly confront controversy and walk together in freedom, always toward the truth of God. Freedom and truth, for Hans Küng, are the pathways by which God reaches us and our way to God. He writes:

> The Church is not a community of the perfect, but is on pilgrimage...toward the ultimate truth. All the false steps, false conclusions, blunders and slips will not ultimately divert the people of God now wandering through many a desert from its destined course.[28]

Ultimately Hans Küng's faith rested in God's ever-present Spirit. That Spirit, likened by Jesus to the wind, has an origin and destination we do not control (John 3:8). Despite any failures, shortcomings, missteps, and abuses we commit as a church, we cannot despair, for the Spirit remains in, with, and among us all. Küng writes:

> It is therefore clear now that...the Spirit of God and of Jesus Christ...is never man's own potential, but the strength, power, gift and grace of God. He is not an unholy spirit of man, spirit of the age, spirit of the Church, spirit of office, spirit of fanaticism. He is and always remains the Holy Spirit of God who breathes where and when he wills and does not permit himself to be claimed as the justification of absolute teaching, and ruling power, of unsubstantiated theology, pious fanaticism and

false security of faith....No church order in teaching and practice, no dogma and no rite compel him now to act and now not to act. God's Spirit is under no law other than that of his own freedom; no justice other than that of his own grace; under no power other than that of his own fidelity....The Church does indeed try continually to take over the Spirit, but it cannot "possess" him, cannot control, restrain, direct or master him.... Despite the continual failure of all its members, the Church has not lost the free Spirit of God.[29]

7. FATHER BERNARD LONERGAN, SJ

THEOLOGIAN AND PHILOSOPHER Bernard Lonergan has left indelible impacts on Catholic philosophy, theology, education, and social thought. While not a self-described "activist," many social activists, laypersons, and clergy have relied on his insights for their theological foundations. Lonergan taught that Catholics should continually expand the horizons of intellectual thought through study and reflection. He believed this work was essential to finding and doing God's will in this world.

In witnessing the spread of Marxism, its decline into totalitarianism in some cases, the Great Depression, and the two horrific world wars, Lonergan was struck by the critical role "ideas" played on the human stage. He therefore sought to understand the origin and impact of ideas, and to view them in light of the reality of Jesus Christ. He therefore studied philosophy, mathematics, and the classics. To understand concrete ways to help the poor, he also studied economics and Catholic social teaching. He considered study and research essential to uncovering our Christian vocation. He once remarked that if a person wanted to help the poor in a substantive way, they should be willing, like Karl Marx, to spend three decades of study in the British Museum. Such was his devotion to sound analysis, correct ideas, and their application to a life committed to the common good.

Lonergan taught theology at the Gregorian Institute, Boston College, and Harvard Divinity School. His voluminous published and unpublished writings can be found in the twenty-seven volumes of *The Collected Works of Bernard Lonergan*.

One of his most significant intellectual contributions was the classic *Method in Theology*. In this work he asserts that while he is devoted to disciplined and scientific study, theology is more of an art than a science. Lonergan presents theology as open and ever-expanding, not a fixed set of formulations that do not and cannot change. For Lonergan, theology, like God, is ever growing, constantly expanding, and continually opening new horizons in our lives. Thus, he notes our theology is the "results of investigation [that] are cumulative and progressive and yield new data, new observations and new descriptions."[30]

Lonergan wrote that the theological method must include a transcendental element. Thus, religion is a part of the theological method and must always include human good and human meaning as a foundation. Further, human good is not an abstract concept but is fulfilled in deeds and practice.

Lonergan does not limit religion and religious belief to a private matter. He writes, "the process of coming to believe what is true is not private but public, not something to be confined to the mind that grasps it, but something independent of the mind and so in a sense is detachable and communicable."[31] Thus, our religious faith is not for us alone, but becomes part of the broader community's common possession, such that we all benefit from what the other has learned or experienced.

He also warns that if in our quest for religious truth we ignore transcendental concepts, the result would be "common nonsense," individual fragmentation, and community alienation. Lonergan wrote that our ability to transcend our limits and pursue our authentic self and values is what promotes individual and community progress. Our quest, therefore, must include a love that transcends self, for he noted, "self-sacrificing love…can undo the mischief of decline and restore cumulative progress."[32]

Love, for Lonergan, is integral to theological reflection and religious practice. He writes:

> Being in love with God, as experienced, is being in love in an unrestricted fashion. All love is self-surrender, but being in love with God is being in love without limits or qualifications or conditions or reservations.[33]

Lonergan fears a religion that does not expand our hearts and minds beyond ourselves and toward the common good. In fact, he notes that faith in "God" that narrows our heart and directs us inward rather than outward can have tragic results, both for individuals and for those who interact with them. In a passage eerily prescient of the dangers of narrow religious fundamentalism, Lonergan writes:

> I have conceived being in love with God as an ultimate fulfillment for man's capacity for self-transcendence; this view of religion is sustained when God is conceived as the supreme fulfillment of transcendental notions, as…truth…reality…goodness. Unless religion is totally directed to what is good, to genuine love of one's neighbor and to a self-denial that is subordinated to a fuller goodness in oneself, then the cult of a God…can slip into the demonic, into an exultant destructiveness of oneself and of others.[34]

Lonergan writes that we are called to "self-transcendence" because God is self-transcending, and our existence, and the world, is the result of God's self-transcendence. Further, "He made us in His image, for our authenticity consists in being like him, in self-transcending."[35] Lonergan helps us understand the meaning of Genesis 1:26, to be created in God's image. For Lonergan, when we transcend self and live among and for others, we become the authentic persons of God's creation. We are called to a life of faith. He writes:

> Without faith, without the eye of love, the world is too evil for God to be good. But faith recognizes that God grants men their freedom, that he wills them to be persons and not just his automata, that he calls them to the higher authenticity that overcomes evil with good. So faith is linked to human progress.[36]

He acknowledges that ours is often a dialectical faith journey, where the tension of opposites guides us forward. The primary tension is our tendency toward self and narrowness on one hand, and our striving for expansiveness, transcendence, and authenticity on the other. On this journey, Lonergan reminds himself and us that "they have to acknowledge their real guilt and amend their ways. They have to learn with humility that religious development is dialectical, that the task of repentance and conversion is lifelong."[37]

Method in Theology, while written for the seminary and the academic world, is a guide for our common journey of faith. Lonergan reminds us that God created us for good, that our authentic self unleashes that good, and that being in love with God and ongoing conversion are essential.

Another of Lonergan's foundational works is the 770-page *Insight,* a philosophical exploration of the foundations of human knowledge and awareness. Convinced that our healing and, indeed, our salvation rest in our awareness, he writes, "To say it with the greatest brevity, one not only has to read *Insight*, but also to discover oneself in oneself."[38] His *The Incarnate Word* explores the person of Christ and applies his unique theory of consciousness to the question of the human Jesus Christ.

Lonergan's writings and lectures have a single goal: to help humans find God and their place in the world. He contends that finding God and our role in life empowers us to work for the common good and the progress of the human family. Thus theologians, religious, priests, and laypersons find inspiration for their faith life and social engagement through the writings of Bernard Lonergan.

> The divine initiative is not just creation. It is not just God's gift of his love. There is a personal entrance of God himself into history, a communication of God to his people....The gift of God's love is matched by his command to love unrestrictedly, with all one's heart and all one's soul and all one's mind and all one's strength....Religious effort toward authenticity through prayer and penance and religious love for all men shown in good deeds become an apostolate.[39]

8. FATHER ENGELBERT MVENG, SJ

ENGELBERT MVENG EXPRESSED his faith in the God of life through word, deed, and art. His art was a consequence of his creativity and his life as a Jesuit priest. Born in Cameroon, Engelbert felt a call to the priesthood and the Society of Jesus at an early age. Employing the teachings of St. Ignatius of Loyola, Mveng found that Ignatian imagination was an essential part of his vocation. St. Ignatius's teachings on imagination emerged from his spiritual illumination alongside the banks of the Cardoner River in 1522. He found that employing our imagination and all our senses when reading the scriptures enables God to speak to us in new ways. Ignatius discovered that placing yourself in a Bible or Gospel narrative can be a source of surprising revelations. For example, when Mary of Bethany anointed Jesus's feet before his arrest and execution (John 12:1–8), readers could imagine themselves in the scene as Lazarus, a disciple, a servant at the dinner, or an unnamed attendee. Ignatius asks that we use our imagination to be aware of the sights and sounds, the energy in the room, the emotions—fear, anger, remorse, sorrow, or joy. What does Jesus look like? Does he notice you? What does he say? Most important for Ignatius, after this reflection, what do you learn about Jesus, God, yourself, your vocation, and others from this prayer? Mveng's artistic expressions exemplify the power of Ignatian imagination. When viewing the art of Father Mveng, it is easy to see how his creative imagination reveals new aspects of God's love.

Mveng's faith was also shaped by Africa's suffering. The woes of the continent are many. Slavery and colonialism left a long shadow. Random national borders drawn in Europe without reference to the various ethnic groups have led to unnecessary conflict. The extraction of wealth and the rise of elites whose priority was personal consumption instead of justice led to riches for a few and poverty for the many. Mveng saw this collective suffering through the eyes of faith and sought to proclaim good news for the poor.

His art combines Ignatian imagination and Africa's pain to convey God's solidarity with the outcast and the suffering. Though Mveng was a scholar of history, theology, and anthropology, his lasting legacies are his artistic expressions. Mveng's art is on display all over the world. His visual interpretations reveal a God whose love draws Him close to our suffering. In Nazareth, the hometown of Jesus Christ, the Basilica of the Annunciation holds his *Our Lady of Africa*. Holy Angels Church in Chicago, Illinois, features his mural revealing angelic activity on behalf of humans throughout all of history. Through Mveng's art, churches, chapels, and education centers around the world convey a message of hope in God's loving presence. Consequently, the prayer lives and social commitments of people the world over are enhanced by Mveng's art.

Hekima College in Nairobi, Kenya, is the theological seminary of the Society of Jesus. The chapel is adorned with Mveng's *Stations of the Cross*. In *The Thirteenth Station* Jesus is taken down from the cross and held in the arms of his mother. This painting expresses Mveng's spirituality as it captures Jesus's solidarity with the oppressed women of Africa. Mary holds Jesus, and Mveng the artist depicts their faces as mirror images of each other, thus conveying Jesus's participation in the sufferings of African women. Mary's dress and Jesus's shroud are the same color, texture, and material, communicating their bond with each other and with each of us. One of the commentators on Mveng's *Thirteenth Station* notes that this painting conveys Africa's unimaginable suffering and death in the context of the reality of God's love. The commentator writes:

> Mveng succeeds in creating a symbol of love and compassion. It is mostly African women who bear the worst repercussions of famine, sickness, and death, while also having to take care of their children (and often losing them). This female experience of mourning for dead offspring suggests something beyond mere biological necessity; it takes us into the realm of religious consciousness. It reveals the power of a love that is "stronger than death" (Song of Solomon 8:6).[40]

The commentator also notes, "Thus, the visual similarity of the faces and bodies of Mary and Jesus in Mveng's painting does more than express their closeness. As Mary's compassion witnesses to this care that will endure beyond death, Mveng transforms the mourning African woman into an *Alter Christus* ('Another Christ')."[41] Mveng does not gloss over or ignore Africa's pain, or the suffering of women. He instead places the very face of Christ over Africa's suffering women. Mveng visually conveys the words of Jesus, "just as you did it to one of the least of these...you did it to me" (Matt 25:40). Jesus in *The Thirteenth Station* was not removed from the cross alone; in reflecting the image of his mother, who in turn represents Africa's suffering women, Jesus is one with the sufferings of the world.

Art was not Mveng's sole expression of faith. He was also the founder of the Movement of African Catholic Intellectuals (MCIA), an organization devoted to utilizing academic research in service of the people. Mveng was also a philosopher, theologian, poet, historian, and priest. His priesthood was one of action, as he was involved in movements to liberate the poor in Cameroon and across the African continent. Like many who follow "the way of the cross," Mveng lost his life for his faith in action. On April 22, 1995, he was brutally murdered in his home in Yaoundé, Cameroon, shortly after he celebrated Mass.

Mveng, like many who side with the poor, was seen as a threat to the status quo, or to any system that promoted private gain over the public good. In a critique of Christian faiths that supported the established and unjust order, he notes, "It is a discourse that claims to tell the truth and produces lies, that claims to speak life and produces death, that claims to speak freedom and produces oppression, that claims to speak equality and produces inequalities, that claims to utter justice and produces injustices."[42]

Despite the continent's suffering, Mveng believed in Africa's openness to spirituality, noting that "[African theology] expresses the faith and hope of our oppressed people. It illustrates the experience of the living Christian communities in Africa. It is therefore not an academic theology, even if some of its promoters move in university circles."[43]

For Mveng, God was not an abstraction but a dynamic center in the daily life of the people. Whether through his art, homilies, intellectual organization, or work among the poor, Mveng's life demonstrated that an experience with God moves us out of ourselves and into the life of the world. Mveng sought to make real the good news of God's Reign. He reminds us all:

> The poor of the Beatitudes are not blessed because they are poor—but because the Reign of God is theirs (Matt 5:1–12). The Lord has not come to institutionalize or beatify misery, but to deliver us from it. That is what Zechariah sings at the beginning

of Luke's Gospel (Luke 1:68–79), that is what the Magnificat proclaims (Luke 1:47–55); that is what the charter of the Beatitudes promulgates (Matt 5:1–12), and that is what the Lord himself reveals in the synagogue at Nazareth, as he inaugurates his public ministry (Luke 4:18–20).[44]

9. FATHER AUGUSTINE (AUGUSTUS) TOLTON

JOHN AUGUSTUS TOLTON was the child of Peter Paul Tolton and Mary Jane Chisley, property of the Hagar family in Ralls County, Missouri. Peter Paul Tolton escaped slavery to fight for the Union, pledging to return and free his beloved wife and children. His wish had no Hollywood ending; we know nothing of his life after he fled enslavement.

Since Missouri was a border state, the enslaved there and in other states close to the North fled bondage across the state lines in hopes of liberty. Mary Jane Chisley, now without a husband, took up that bold course of action. One evening, she spirited her children out of bed and tiptoed past the armed guards and snarling plantation dogs. Securing a small boat, she rowed across the Mississippi River. Unarmed, unable to swim, drawing strength from her dream of liberty, she dodged bullets and curses to protect her children as she rowed. Her boat reached the free soil of Illinois, and she guided her children to safety. Neither she nor her pursuers knew that one of the children in that boat would later become the first African American Catholic priest in the United States.

When she was enslaved, Mary Jane had been baptized, along with her children, by a priest in Ralls County. Her son John Augustus was christened Augustine. Mary Jane's faith sustained her as she struggled to provide food and shelter for her children in Quincy, Illinois. Mary Jane enrolled her son Augustine in St. Boniface School. Like all Black Catholics of that era, he learned that faith did not end racism among his white Catholic classmates. He was verbally abused, harassed, and often threatened by children who learned racism from their parents.

Despite these perversions of the faith, young Augustine found God in the Catholic Church, along with the love and peace so lacking in the world. When he was sixteen years old, Augustine told Father Peter McGirr of St. Peter's parish that he wanted to become a Catholic priest. Father McGirr and other local priests were impressed with his sincerity and assisted his quest, but no American seminaries were accepting Black candidates for the priesthood. Undeterred, Augustine worked in a tobacco factory and as a church custodian and saloon janitor to save money for his dream.

He continued his academic formation at the high school within St. Francis College in Quincy. During lessons on St. Thomas Aquinas's *Summa Theologiae* and Aquinas's views on justice, Augustine said,

> I know about slavery....Oh, tell me, where does justice come in?...I cannot tell you how deeply I feel for my race. What is the use of studying about justice? Why don't we do something about it?... How can a dehumanized person have responsibility? And, each of us has one life to live, and we can't wait. We are ready now to receive justice and equality, opportunity and religion.[45]

As a lay member of St. Joseph's parish in Quincy, Tolton was often found among both the Black and white residents of the town, encouraging them to attend Sunday school or Mass. He also spoke with men in bars and saloons about joining the Temperance Society, of which he was a regular member. Father Michael Richardt, OFM, spoke of his work among Black residents of Quincy saying:

> I could not have accomplished a thing without his help, because I was wholly unacquainted with Negroes....Augustine was instrumental in getting the children to attend Sunday school...later he encouraged adults to come also....In fact Augustine Tolton was an energizing force not only for his race but for me as well.[46]

As he tirelessly engaged the struggling people of Quincy, Augustine Tolton later wrote, "I wish I were a priest and could do something for them, I could bring them forgiveness and grace and strength, I could help people to become better."[47]

After years of rejection letters from U.S. seminaries, his small network of supportive priests encouraged him to apply in Rome where race could be less a factor. They were right, and in 1880, Tolton announced to his overjoyed mother that he was going to Rome to study to become a priest. He later said his time at the Collegium Urbanum de Propaganda de Fide in Rome was a time of full and complete human happiness. Tolton was ordained a Roman Catholic priest at St. John Lateran on April 24, 1886. Hands that worked on a Missouri plantation were anointed by Cardinal Parocchi to pray, heal, and celebrate the sacraments.

After experiencing the hate and violence of racism in America, Father Augustine Tolton hoped for an assignment in Africa. The church, however, wanted him to return home and serve in the United States.

He was sent to the bishop of Illinois, where he was asked to serve St. Joseph parish in Quincy, Illinois. Confirming his initial fears, Tolton was opposed by fellow priests, local Protestants, and even his own parish. Despite repeatedly asking them to refrain from derogatory references, his own parishioners referred to him as "our nigger priest."

His devotion to Christ alone strengthened him in his duties. He believed his calling and gifts were suited to serve a Black community and parish. Thus, aware of the Black Catholic presence in Chicago, Tolton requested assignment to an African American parish there.

Chicago was home to St. Mary's Church, considered the cradle of Black Catholicism in Chicago. St. Mary's eventually moved to a storefront that became the new St. Monica's parish. St. Monica's requested Tolton as their pastor, and the bishop agreed, thus beginning a partnership between America's first Black priest and Chicago's oldest Black parish.

His calling took him beyond the parish and into the surrounding neighborhood. He spoke with people on the street corners, visited tenements, and, as in Quincy, went to places where people drowned despair with alcohol. All around the parish were poverty and desperation. Father Tolton later said, "These poor people have been left in a bag with both ends open."[48] He and the parish sought to offer hope and dignity to the oppressed Blacks of Chicago's south side. His sister and mother later joined him in Chicago.

In 1889, lay leader Daniel Rudd called together the Colored Catholic Congress, the first Black Catholic gathering in the United States. This assembly later became the National Black Catholic Congress, a body that continues to meet every five years. At the first meeting in 1889, Father Tolton was the main speaker. The periodical *Our Colored Missions* notes that Father Tolton often proclaimed to his audiences:

> The Catholic church deplores double slavery—that of the mind and that of the body. She endeavors to free us of both....When the Church does all of this, is she not the true liberator of the race? In

> this Church we do not have to fight for our rights because we are black. She had colored saints—Saint Augustine, St. Benedict the Moor, Saint Monica....She is the church for our people.[49]

Like Daniel Rudd and other Black Catholics of that era, Father Tolton looked beyond the practices of white Catholics to grasp and hold the promises of Jesus Christ.

Many recalled Tolton going from apartment to apartment, a constant figure in the streets and alleys of the neighborhood, listening, praying, giving, and serving. Tolton died on July 9, 1897, of heatstroke and uremia, both conditions brought on by his tireless work. He lived the answer to a question he asked one of his priest mentors in his early years: "Can anyone spread Christianity by being unchristian?"[50] His answer was then, and for the rest of his life, a resounding *no*. He was a Christian, a follower of Christ, in Quincy, in Rome, and in the streets, alleys, and tenements of Chicago. Tolton said yes to freedom, yes to Christ, and yes to the priesthood and a lifetime of service.

PART IV

BISHOPS AND CARDINALS

Bishops should present Christ's teaching in a manner relevant to the needs of the times, providing a response to those difficulties and problems which people find especially distressing and burdensome.

Decree on the Pastoral Office of Bishops in the Church,
Christus Dominus 13

1. CARDINAL PAULO EVARISTO ARNS, OFM

PAULO EVARISTO ARNS served as bishop and cardinal of Sao Paulo, Brazil, from 1970 to 1988. Brazil, home to the world's largest Catholic population, was a land of contradictions and conflict. On one hand, the military dictatorship routinely arrested, tortured, and sometimes murdered political opponents, human rights activists, and other Brazilian citizens. On the other hand, activists, reformers, and Catholics influenced by liberation theology's "preferential option for the poor" worked for systemic change. Cardinal Arns saw solidarity with the poor as a fundamental call of the Gospel. At Cardinal Arns's ninety-fifth birthday celebration, his former press secretary, Fernando Altemeyer, told the hundreds in attendance, "When Brazil was plunged into darkness, Dom Paulo was the star that illuminated it."[1] In citing the image of a "star," Altemeyer alluded to Jesus's comments: "You are the light of the world....No one after lighting a lamp puts it under the bushel basket, but on the lampstand, and it gives light to all in the house" (Matt 5:14–15). Arns was the lamp in Brazil's darkness.

The military dictatorship in Brazil ruled by force, terror, and fear. While many Christians in North America see "religious freedom" as liberty to discriminate against LGTBQ people or the right to bear arms, in Brazil, many people of faith understood that "freedom" as an obligation to serve rather than assertion of personal rights. As followers of Jesus, they confronted violent powers in their quest to practice a faith of justice and mercy. They understood that the Gospel of Jesus Christ was diametrically opposed to the values of private accumulation, impoverishment of the masses, and violent enforcement of inequality. Living the words of Jesus Christ, their primary concern was to enlighten the darkness of Brazilian society with the light of God's love, mercy, and justice.

Cardinal Arns was a powerful voice at the 1968 conference of Latin American bishops at Medellín. At a time when the world's global powers attempted to force all nations to choose America's capitalism or the Soviet Union's socialism, he sought justice. Choosing instead liberation theology's "preferential option for the poor," he stated, "I was never in favor of capitalism or communism, [I wanted] a social system where all would have what is sufficient for a decent life and where there would be justice and equality. In our country 2 percent of the population has more wealth than the other 95 percent. This is a scandal."[2] Arns's words echoed the sentiments of Pope Paul VI's 1967 *Populorum Progressio,* his encyclical that urged Catholics to work for "integral human development" and an economy that served not a few but all. The document, if practiced, would place the church squarely in the struggle for the dignity, development, and freedom of every human person.

In 1973, Arns was elevated to cardinal by Pope Paul VI. For Arns, nothing was more destructive to human dignity than a government that creates fear and sustains inequality through arrest, torture, and murder. The dictatorship was in power from 1964 to 1985 and left a trail of human rights abuses. Its leaders came to power by the overthrow of a reformist government and were backed by the military apparatus, the Catholic Church, the economic elite, and the United States. Though the coup initially included moderate and conservative elements, hardliners eventually eased out the more centrist voices and took control of the government. They were influenced by Washington's "National Security Doctrine," which affirmed it was the responsibility of the military to "avoid political polarization" (interpreted as destroying leftist opposition) and "counter the actions of communist infiltrators" (essentially, anyone who supported labor or the poor was a suspected communist). The Brazilian military pursued this doctrine with a vengeance.

Through accusation, misinformation, and rumors, the government targeted and arrested many who stood alongside the poor. Many others were tortured and murdered. In 1975, a journalist who exposed the dark side of Brazil was murdered, a death the government called "suicide." Arns and other religious leaders spoke out against his murder and issued a pastoral letter condemning the violence.

In 1979, labor leader Santo Dias Da Silva was murdered by the military police. Cardinal Arns marched into the morgue to retrieve the body, waving away the police who attempted to block his entry. Upon viewing the bullet holes in Da Silva's body, Arns scolded the officers, shouting, "Look at what you did!" Confronted by the cardinal, the officers are reported to have lowered their heads in shame.[3]

Arns and other leaders of the Catholic Church were also engaged in empowering the poor to work for their own "integral human development." Arns, Bishop Dom Helder Camara, and Bishop Pedro Casaldáliga were active in pastoral work among the poor and in creating the base communities of Brazil. These formations were the practical application of liberation theology in the lives of the people. In these communities, laypersons, the poor, workers, the unemployed, and others met together, studied the scriptures, analyzed social conditions, and implemented strategies to bring dignity, security, and hope to the common people of Brazil. Often women were the leaders in these base communities.

Arns's engagement with liberation theology also took him to Rome to defend Father Leonardo Boff, under investigation by the Congregation for the Doctrine of the Faith, led by future Pope Benedict XVI, then Cardinal Ratzinger. While the Vatican supported Arns's opposition to human rights abuses, they believed his advocacy for the poor through liberation theology went too far.

The Vatican was not alone, for the Brazilian government considered Arns an enemy, and the most powerful nation on earth, the United States, saw him as "a leftist." For them, solidarity with the poor and demands for economic justice were smokescreens for communist infiltration. Consequently, in their Cold War mentality, there was a communist behind every labor strike, every base community, and every demand for jobs, literacy, or land.

Though facing powerful forces, Arns stood firm; he sheltered labor leaders, advocated for workers' rights, led base communities, spoke out against repression, and even built a small radio station next to his home to expose the excesses of the secret police. In 1983 he was invited to a bishops' meeting on the theme "Reconciliation and Penance." Rather than focus on personal piety, Arns insisted the meeting include a time for the church leaders to ask themselves, "Who confesses the economic sins committed against the third world?"[4] In 1985 he published a book, *Brasil, Nunca Mais* (*Brazil, Never Again*), that cataloged and condemned the widespread use of torture by the military. Arns recognized that social revolutions, even when flawed in their overall governance, could yield economic, health, educational, and other benefits to the masses. He wrote, "Christian faith discovers in the achievements of revolution signs of the kingdom of God."[5] For this activist cardinal, political revolutions were not substitutes for God's reign, but they could, with integrity, faith, and solidarity, create a more human life for all.

Year after year Arns sought to make God's reign a reality despite repression and poverty. He continued to be a light in the darkness. In his tireless work for justice and human rights, he made the love of God a reality in Brazil. There are thousands of anonymous Brazilians—Indigenous, poor, of African descent, women, labor leaders, and others, who were enlightened, empowered, and transformed by the courageous works of Cardinal Evaristo Arns.

> In the time when Brazil was living a cruel dictatorship, he always spoke and spoke loudly against torture, against violations of human rights and the lack of freedoms that were taken by the dictatorship.[6]

2. BISHOP PEDRO CASALDÁLIGA, CMF

MATTHEW FOX'S BOOK *The Pope's War: Why Cardinal Ratzinger's Secret Crusade Has Imperiled the Church and How It Can Be Saved* includes the investigation of Bishop Pedro Casaldáliga of Brazil. Casaldáliga was one of the many Latin American leaders and theologians who were suspected of beliefs and practices contrary to Catholic teaching. Some viewed liberation theology and solidarity with the poor as more Marxist than Catholic. Matthew Fox notes that in 1971, deep in the Amazon jungle, Bishop Casaldáliga wrote a poem on a wild banana leaf with his pocketknife. The poem, "Cry of the Soul," was popular for years among Brazil's poor as a national anthem, a dirge, and a celebration.[7] In the poem he expresses his Catholic faith, noting that everyone in Brazil, particularly the poor, belong to the people of God who already have a place in heaven and who seek a just home here on earth.

Casaldáliga spoke out for the millions of landless peasants, many of whom were forced from their ancestral lands through the exploitation of the Amazon rainforest. Casaldáliga centered the peasants' hope on God while at the same time demanding their full rights as Brazilian citizens and as the people of God. Heavenly citizenship demands that justice and mercy be done on earth. Therefore, the good news is not about the hereafter alone but more about the here and now.

Casaldáliga was born in Spain in 1928, joined the priesthood, and in 1968 moved to Brazil as a Claretian missionary.

Upon arrival, he saw the impacts of poverty on the lives of the people. Thus, as a missionary, priest, and later bishop, Casaldáliga preached both the gospel of salvation and the good news of a better life. He lived with and among the people, and thus knew well the cruelty brought upon Indigenous peoples, landless peasants, women, and Black Brazilians. Author Penny Lernoux describes him: "A short wisp of a man with the courage of a martyr, Dom Pedro is typical of the fighting bishops of Brazil…leaders of the world's largest Catholic Church and in many ways its most progressive."[8]

Casaldáliga was bishop of the Sao Felix Diocese, which included part of the Amazon rainforest. The Indigenous people of that region had been fighting for their existence for years against international mining companies supported by the Brazilian military dictatorships that extracted local resources for private gain. Life for Indigenous people was difficult, for they not only lost their ancestral lands but sometimes faced violent suppression from company militias and Brazilian soldiers.

Casaldáliga was one of the hundreds of Catholic bishops, priests, religious, and laypeople whose faith was inspired by Vatican II and who were moved to action by liberation theology. Their social works inspired by their faith did not go unnoticed, for in Brazil and other Latin American nations, over 850 Catholic leaders are estimated to have been murdered by the government, police, or death squads.

Casaldáliga once went to a local police station with a priest to demand release of two local women who were being tortured and abused. During the discussions with the police, the priest, Father João Burnier, was shot dead while standing next to the bishop. Such was the violence endured by the poor. This was not an isolated incident, for Casaldáliga himself and the Catholics and poor of his diocese were often subject to death threats from land barons, large-scale miners, loggers, corporate interests, and the government.

As bishop, Casaldáliga organized peasant cooperatives, helped establish school and health units, and taught the poor their rights and how to defend them. He and those in his diocese constantly explored new ways to worship, to communicate, and to collaborate so the community could live with dignity. His provincial superior, Claretian father Marcos Loro, described his work by noting:

> The congregation and the church received a great gift from God in the person and work of Pedro, who was a man of fidelity, coherence and conduct that united faith and practice. He used to say he lived in the Valley of the Forgotten and sought from government agencies justice for the indigenous and the poor. He made the church more present in the [Amazon] region and gave voice to the laymen in the communities.[9]

In 1988, after several inquiries and investigations, Bishop Casaldáliga was silenced by Cardinal Ratzinger and the Congregation for the Doctrine of the Faith. He was charged with writing favorably about liberation theology, supporting a Nicaraguan hunger strike, allowing a Mass to be centered on Black and Indigenous culture, and calling slain archbishop Oscar Romero a "martyr."

Casaldáliga's silencing meant he could not mention liberation theology and speak or say Mass in other countries without permission from Rome, but the restrictions could not stop the bishop from Brazil. While he could not "mention" liberation theology, he could live it through active work among the poor. Casaldáliga was not silent about his penalty. He later wrote:

> Obeying the pope and the bishops doesn't mean keeping your mouth shut in their presence; like little children who have no responsibility, and simply accepting everything they say or do. In the church we should be adults. We are all church, holy and sinful....Vatican Council II has providentially rediscovered that the church is the People of God, gathered in Christ. A people journeying toward full liberation.[10]

He saw the journey toward liberation as a fundamental aspect of being the church. It was not a path to be walked alone but alongside others. He wrote, "This awareness of Being Church should fill us with gratitude, responsibility and freedom of spirit which should enable us to live it with greater awareness, freedom and reality."[11] For Casaldáliga, a sense of freedom and responsibility helped him realize that as much as he loved the Catholic Church, his fidelity to God, Jesus Christ, and the Gospel superseded his loyalty to an institution. Though silenced, he nonetheless continued to serve and love the people of his diocese. The Brazilian bishop's Land Commission said that his life is an example for all who fight for justice and democracy anywhere in the world. When El Salvadoran archbishop Oscar Romero was murdered, Casaldáliga wrote a poem saying Romero knew how to drink the chalice of the altar, and of the people. That poem affirmed Romero's and Casaldáliga's devotion to the eucharistic offering of Christ's life for the world, and the presence of Christ in the people of the world.

Mystic, prophet, poet, bishop, activist, Bishop Pedro Casaldáliga died at age ninety-two in 2020. His funeral mirrored his life. When describing his funeral, Claretian father Ronaldo Mazula told the *National Catholic Reporter*:

> Casaldáliga was placed barefoot in a simple coffin covered with a patchwork shawl from Nicaragua and a cross on his chest made by the Xavante Indians for the vigil in the city of Batatais....The Claretian chapel was adorned with burned logs to represent the death of the forest and barbed wire to represent landowners. Also, near the altar where the bishop lay, church workers placed indigenous artifacts and Victoria Regia, a giant water lily common in the Amazon region, to represent the priest's actions in favor of the environment and the indigenous.[12]

Even in death, Bishop Casaldáliga's fidelity to the Gospel of life and commitment to the Indigenous and the poor inspired all in attendance to continue his work. Fellow archbishop Leonardo Ulrich Steiner wrote,

> He made the church realize that we cannot abandon the poor....He himself was poor; he lived like his followers, in poverty, I know this because I lived with him for seven years in a very simple house in the middle of the community. He lived with those he helped, with the poor.[13]

3. BISHOP THOMAS GUMBLETON

AUXILIARY BISHOP THOMAS Gumbleton of Detroit has often said that in order to resist violence with nonviolence, we need commitment, training, and above all, a conviction that the way of love is the only road to true peace. For Bishop Gumbleton, those words are a calling, a way of life, a vocation.

By the time he was ordained a bishop of Detroit in 1968, he had already acquired a reputation for courage, insight, and pastoral care when addressing social issues. As a priest serving inner-city neighborhoods in Detroit, he lived in poor communities and was an outspoken advocate for those on the margins. Gumbleton believed that God's reign enveloped the whole of life, transforming our personal life, social life, and politics by the light of Christ.

Two events opened his eyes and heart to a wider view of justice. First was Vatican II and its aftermath. He writes:

> [Vatican II] brought a lot of changes in my own ministry. After the council...social justice came to the forefront as a constitutive element of preaching the Gospel. That meant involvement in the social structures of the world, trying to transform them to represent what God wanted for humankind.[14]

The second incident that shaped his vocation was a trip he and two other priests took to the Holy Land. He said they "began to come into a large area teeming with homeless people...living in the streets all the time, without access to water, food, or any clean clothing.... Sooner or later, I knew I would have to act upon what I had experienced there."[15]

Holding those pivotal events close to his heart, Bishop Gumbleton devoted himself to justice and peace. He traveled the world, calling for an end to war and a halt to nuclear weapons. He became a persistent voice for peace, negotiations, dialogue, and above all, love in action. He was one of the first bishops to speak out against the Vietnam War. Gumbleton believed that the Vietnam War was unjust, unnecessary, and an extension of white colonialism.

In 1972 he and other Catholics and Protestants founded Pax Christi USA, an American ecumenical peace movement. Pax Christi continues as a voice for safe immigration, racial awareness and justice, and peace on the streets and in the world. In 1974 he and other people of faith began Bread for the World. Since its founding, Bread for the World has strengthened nutrition programs and drastically reduced hunger in the United States. The organization has also lobbied for international assistance from wealthier nations to enhance access to healthy food for millions in Latin America, Asia, and Africa.

During the 1979 Iran hostage crisis, Gumbleton led a delegation to meet with the hostages in Tehran. Four years later, when the Reagan administration was bellowing rhetoric about nuclear weapons and space wars, Bishop Gumbleton coauthored the 1983 U.S. Conference of Catholic Bishops Pastoral Letter, "The Challenge of Peace: God's Promise, Our Response." That document condemned the proliferation and use of nuclear weapons. Section 58 noted:

> Christians are called to live the tension between the vision of the reign of God and its concrete realization in history. The tension is often described in terms of "already but not yet": i.e., we already

> live in the grace of the kingdom, but it is not yet the completed kingdom. Hence, we are a pilgrim people in a world marked by conflict and injustice.[16]

The document also boldly proclaimed in section 333:

> In the words of our Holy Father, we need a "moral about face." The whole world must summon the moral courage and technical means to say "no" to nuclear conflict; "no" to weapons of mass destruction; "no" to an arms race which robs the poor and the vulnerable; and "no" to the moral danger of a nuclear age which places before humankind indefensible choices of constant terror or surrender. Peacemaking is not an optional commitment. It is a requirement of our faith.[17]

Under Gumbleton's leadership, the bishops called for negotiations, an end to the arms race, and cessation of talk of "first strike," "preemptive strikes," and any language that endangered millions of human lives and, perhaps, all of life forms on the planet.

With the rise in gun violence in the United States, Gumbleton believed the work of Pax Christi extended to that issue as well. In an interview acknowledging the fiftieth anniversary of Pax Christi, Gumbleton noted:

> It seems to me that since we started 50 years ago in the U.S., that violence has increased enormously, the number of shootings in malls and schools or almost anywhere—the recent one in Texas where all those children were murdered—so that sort of thing has happened more and more. The violence

> in our country just seems to be getting more and more out of control.[18]

He also spoke of what he has learned from his engagement in Pax Christi:

> Within the movement we put a major influence on the act of love or nonviolence, and then, in my own life, I went through a very profound conversion to that. Because I grew up, as Catholics did generally, with a conviction that war could be justified. It was through Pax Christi that I came to understand that, within the teachings of Jesus, war cannot be justified. So Pax Christi, in my life, helped to bring about a profound conversion away from any acts of violence for any reason whatsoever and toward only making peace through active love or nonviolence, and that was a major change in my life....War is never justified.[19]

Bishop Gumbleton has met with victims of war in Iraq, Afghanistan, Vietnam, El Salvador, Nicaragua, Guatemala, Israel, Palestine, Colombia, Haiti, and Peru. These face-to-face meetings fueled his passion for peace; victims are not statistics or numbers, but real suffering humans. He has held malnourished Haitian babies, Afghan children whose limbs were blown off, and survivors of Salvadoran villages whose homes and friends were incinerated by U.S.-made explosives.

He has also been outspoken for the rights of LGTBQ people, the empowerment of women, and support for the victims of priest abuse. In each of these cases, he spoke out despite opposition and silence from many in the Catholic hierarchy. For Gumbleton, the Gospel of Jesus Christ is more compelling than political ideology and social pressure.

In 1990 he went to Iraq to try and prevent the first Gulf War. Thirteen years later he opposed the invasion of Iraq. Unlike many who were duped by the "smoking gun in the form of a mushroom cloud" rhetoric and the lies regarding Saddam Hussein and 9/11, Gumbleton saw that invasion for what it was: unjust, unnecessary, and destabilizing.

In a homily on the Feast of Corpus Christi, Bishop Gumbleton noted that Jesus asked us to do two specific things. He asked that in the Eucharist we "do this in memory of me." Jesus also asked that we "wash each other's feet." He noted that Catholics speak reverently of the "Real Presence" and the importance of the Eucharist, yet we are less enthusiastic about Jesus's clear demand that we "do this"—love as we have been loved. Gumbleton wrote, "The Eucharist isn't a thing, it's an action,"[20] an act of mercy we carry from the altar to the world.

4. ARCHBISHOP RAYMOND HUNTHAUSEN

AS A CHILD, RAYMOND HUNTHAUSEN wanted to be a fighter pilot, husband, father, and lifetime resident of his native Montana. God had other plans. In a vocation much different from air combat, Raymond Hunthausen, as archbishop of Seattle, led peaceful protests against the nuclear submarines stationed within his diocese. Anything that diminished human life was his concern, and the bishop was an outspoken supporter of health care, racial equality, dignity for LGTBQ people, and women's rights.

His journey from daydreamer fighter pilot to peacemaking bishop was marked by significant encounters. Among them were Bishop Bernard Topel's encouragement to deepen his spiritual life and seek ordination, his attendance at Vatican II, and his encounter with James Douglass and the Pacific Life Community. After many years of service as a priest, Hunthausen was surprised when the Vatican appointed him bishop of Montana. Then forty-one, he became the youngest bishop in the United States. A few weeks after his ordination as a bishop, Hunthausen attended the largest gathering in human history, the ecumenical council known as Vatican II. The council, called by Pope John XXIII, radically transformed the Roman Catholic Church, a global institution with a two-thousand-year history.

The transformative power of Vatican II is difficult to overestimate; it energized the liturgy, empowered the laity, opened the scriptures, called on the Holy Spirit, and changed the church from a triumphant hierarchy to the pilgrim people of God. As a young bishop, Hunthausen embodied the spirit of the council. His biographer John McCoy writes:

> He had a new idea of his role as a bishop, as a servant leader who convenes, collaborates, and inspires rather than dictates, reprimands and proscribes, and he had a new vision of his Catholic faith in which Christ liberates and loves all—regardless of their beliefs or their sins—especially the poor, the suffering, the abandoned and the victims of war and injustice.[21]

Hunthausen later confirmed, "For me to have attempted to be a bishop without the council would have been a disaster, my goodness, the spirit and theology of the council turned my head around."[22] In Helena, Montana, he created a priest senate, parish and diocesan councils, opportunities for the laity to voice their issues, and other instruments of empowerment. Thirteen years later he was appointed the archbishop of the Diocese of Seattle.

While archbishop of Seattle, Hunthausen met James Douglass of the Pacific Life Community (PLC). Douglass was a committed pacifist, and the PLC a collection of Quakers, feminists, and Catholic Workers who worked to end war, the nuclear arms race, and "the personal violence in their own lives."[23] This encounter sparked the archbishop's commitment to eliminating nuclear weapons.

In Seattle, Hunthausen continually expanded his vision of the church as bearer of Christ's peace on earth. In ecclesiastical, political, and social circles he spoke out for justice and inclusion. Hunthausen backed his words with marches and sit-ins, and in an act of further civil disobedience, withheld that portion of his taxes that funded nuclear weapons. He noted to his fellow bishops:

> If God is the ultimate source of our solace and safety, how can we make nuclear weapons the absolute basis for our security? Nuclear deterrence is idolatry…in our proclamation of the Gospel, it is the cross, the power of Christ, who is the savior of the world.[24]

Hunthausen disagreed with the exclusion of women from the diaconate program and from other leadership positions in the church. He therefore abolished the diaconate in his diocese and utilized the position of pastoral life director (PLD) to appoint women to leadership roles. Hunthausen called women as PLDs to be pastors and leaders in local parishes. I attended a Seattle parish, St. Therese, pastored by Patty Repikoff, whose leadership is in large part responsible for my conversion to Catholicism. Priests from around the diocese and from the Jesuit-run Seattle University collaborated by celebrating the Eucharist with the female pastors. Bishop Hunthausen also held ecumenical services with other faith traditions and welcomed LGBTQ meetings in local parishes.

Like other progressive theologians, nuns, bishops, and priests, Hunthausen attracted the attention of the Congregation for the Doctrine of the Faith with his ministry. Headed by Cardinal Ratzinger, the congregation considered itself the protector of Catholic tradition, thought, and practice. Its investigation of Hunthausen began with a cryptic message informing him that he would be subject to a papal "visitation." The visitation would end up lasting years and include investigations, threats, and mischaracterizations. He was accused of ignoring the Catholic "just war" teaching, allowing priests who left the priesthood to marry and continue teaching, openly discussing women's ordination, and other heretical misdeeds. Of all the charges, the most "egregious" were his opposition to the nuclear buildup and his dialogue with gays and lesbians.

This investigation, which later became known in Catholic circles as "the Hunthausen Affair," came to a head when the bishop was summoned to Rome to meet with Cardinal Ratzinger. The cardinal questioned why he welcomed the gay organization, Dignity, into the diocesan cathedral. Hunthausen responded with Jesus's encounter with the accusers of the woman caught in adultery. Jesus told the crowd primed to stone the woman, "Let anyone among you who is without sin be the first to throw a stone at her" (John 8:7). Ratzinger interrupted, "Are you presuming to lecture me?" Hunthausen continued, only to be told by Ratzinger, "Don't preach to me."[25]

The investigation continued with reports and accusations that Hunthausen was never allowed to review. Vatican-appointed "co-bishops" were sent to watch and counter decisions made by the archbishop, and public announcements undermined his authority. The Seattle community and most of the diocese rallied around their archbishop.

Eventually, Donald Wuerl was appointed auxiliary bishop with confusing roles and authority. This was difficult for both men. Their conflict can be summed up in a description by a canon lawyer on the chancery staff who noted that while Wuerl perceived people and issues as either inside or outside the box, Hunthausen didn't see a box at all.

Years of investigations, reports, meetings, and charges created stress and anger within the Diocese of Seattle. During the visitation, one of his supporters asked if he still loved the church. Bishop Hunthausen said he did, and that the greatest of all theologies is the theology of struggle. That struggle would end with Hunthausen's resignation. In 1991, after sixteen years of service, he left his role as archbishop of Seattle. Addressing his staff and supporters in his final speech, Hunthausen said, "I have come to see myself as someone who was invited to be a leader, invited to join a struggle to be faithful to the Gospel."[26] His biographer adds:

> Vatican II resonated deeply with his hopes for a church that would transform lives and the world. He left the council "born again," convinced that we are all "People of God" called to "share responsibility" in building the kingdom of God in this world, not the next.…The council taught him, he said, that the church is *semper reformanda,* always in need of reform. That means we are to continually examine our own hearts and minds as we seek to understand God's will for us today.[27]

No visitation, investigation, charge, or accusation could drive Hunthausen away from his faith. How utterly criminal, that while the Congregation for the Doctrine of the Faith was investigating a peace activist, the hierarchy ignored and enabled the priest sexual abuse scandal that ruined lives, demolished Catholic credibility, and cost millions of dollars. May the legacy of Hunthausen remind us that God is not found in hierarchical structures and self-proclaimed gatekeepers but in the People of God called to live for truth, mercy, justice, and peace.

5. CARDINAL JAIME LACHICA SIN

FROM 1965 TO 1986, President Ferdinand Marcos ruled the Philippines in an antidemocratic, repressive, and corrupt regime. Marcos was one of the many dictators who enjoyed support of the most powerful nation on earth, the United States. These leaders were noted for their repression of leftists and the poor, rampant corruption, and enrichment of the few.

In the midst of political repression were communities of faith that had to choose between acquiescence or resistance. In 1974 Father Jaime Lachica Sin was named bishop of Manila and faced the tension of proclaiming the good news of Jesus Christ while surrounded by the bad news of injustice. In a predominantly Catholic society, the bishop of Manila is one of the most visible Catholic leaders in the Philippines. His comments and actions signal to the faithful the most appropriate Catholic response to political and economic realities. Bishop Sin chose a middle path, gently defending the poor while muting his criticism of the government. He called his middle path "critical collaboration."[28] He also believed he could create change through negotiation with the Marcos government. Bishop Sin soon saw the limits of accommodation when the military invaded a Manila seminary in "search of insurgents." In addition, he saw how government repression impacted the lives of the people in his diocese.

Bishop Sin was elevated to cardinal by Pope Paul VI in 1976, the third Filipino cardinal in Catholic Church history. Jaime Sin, at forty-eight-years old, was the spiritual head of forty million Filipino Catholics. The tension between faith and political realities continued, as Marcos's martial law and other policies increased misery among the masses. Every week revealed new tales of injustice and corruption. Like Archbishop Romero of El Salvador, Cardinal Sin moved from accommodation to solidarity and resistance. He boldly and prophetically denounced the excesses of the Marcos regime. Due to his critique of the flagrant opulence of Imelda Marcos, Ferdinand's wife, she declared him a "communist homosexual."[29] In an age when either of those labels could mean condemnation, arrest, or even murder, that was an incendiary charge. Still, Cardinal Sin continued his criticism in support of the suffering masses of Filipinos.

The tension between faith and injustice would burst asunder with the return from exile of Benigno "Ninoy" Aquino in 1983. A former senator and opponent of Ferdinand Marcos, Aquino was arrested years earlier on false charges and jailed for seven years. In need of medical attention, he was exiled to the United States in 1980. In 1983, he returned to the Philippines to negotiate peace with Marcos and perhaps open the door for free and fair elections. This was not to be. On August 21, 1983, Aquino's plane landed in Manila. Before the rest of the passengers disembarked, he was led off the plane by armed security guards. Once he reached the bottom of the stairs, Aquino was murdered, shot in the head by his "escorts." This brazen and public murder was Marcos's message that no opposition or challenge would be tolerated.

Cardinal Sin, as leader of the Philippine Catholic Church, embraced the mantle of Amos, Jeremiah, Micah, and the other Hebrew prophets who spoke God's truth to unjust political powers. When Benigno's wife, Corazon Aquino, returned home and was embraced by the people as a potential leader, Cardinal Sin supported her. He led the

Catholic Church to consider Benigno's murder and Corazon's rise as a reenactment of the *pasyon*, the passion of Christ.[30] That image saw Benigno as Christ crucified for the people and Corazon as Mary showing the people the way to resurrection and salvation.

For Cardinal Sin and the people, the metaphor of the *pasyon* fueled the "people power" movement where common Filipinos rose up as a resurrected people to oppose Marcos's dictatorship. Marcos realized the threat of Corazon Aquino's presence and thus restricted her ability to speak, write, or connect with the people. Cardinal Jaime Sin became her public voice, and he used his pulpit, the newspapers, and the radio to raise her profile in opposition to Marcos. Buoyed by faith in God and the knowledge that millions standing together could not be ignored, Sin showed that the good news of Christ was a reality.

He urged the people to stand as one, warning that "it is possible we are becoming a nation of sheep."[31] His reference to "sheep" was laden with meanings easily understood by the Catholic population. Familiar with Jesus's discourse on the Good Shepherd, the people knew the sheep were those Jesus had warned were faced with bandits and thieves intent to "steal, kill and destroy." Jesus also warned of uncaring hired hands who ran away and let the lurking wolves scatter and snatch the sheep. However, Jesus spoke of another outcome; when the sheep heard the voice of the Good Shepherd, they could follow him toward abundant life (John 10:1–14). Cardinal Sin subtly contrasted thieves, bandits, and wolves (Marcos and his cronies) with the guiding love of the Good Shepherd (Jesus and those who hear and follow him).

The defining moment of Cardinal Sin's ministry came when three hundred officers publicly broke with Marcos and took refuge inside military headquarters. Among them was former defense minister Juan Ponce Enrile. Realizing that

Marcos would not hesitate to massacre them, Ponce called Cardinal Sin begging him to intervene. He told the cardinal that without help, they would be dead within the hour. Cardinal Sin faced a serious dilemma. As a cardinal, his intervention could be seen as the church's direct involvement in a perceived military coup. In addition, the Vatican opposed his further involvement. On the other hand, silence could mean a massacre and untold misery for millions. Cardinal Sin began to pray, fervently but quickly, for an answer. He heard God call him to act, and the cardinal went on the airwaves that evening urging the people to engage in massive non-violent demonstrations. His defiance of the Vatican and the dictator resulted in two million Filipinos flooding the streets of Manila and standing between the three hundred officers and the amassed military of Ferdinand Marcos. By the second day of demonstrations, Marcos ordered the troops to fire on the protestors. They refused as nuns placed rosaries in front of tanks and the people put flowers in machine guns and rifles. Images of the nonviolent protests were broadcast all over the world.[32] The protests continued for three days, and People Power prevailed, forcing Marcos to leave office and flee to Hawaii. Incredibly, no shots were fired, and Cardinal Sin declared the event a miracle. In that critical moment, with a massacre and destruction looming, Cardinal Sin echoed Peter and the apostles when they continued to preach after being ordered to keep silent. As Peter declared, "We must obey God rather than any human authority" (Acts 5:29).

Corazon Aquino was elected president of the Philippines in 1986, and Cardinal Sin was her close advisor and an advocate for the needs of the people. The people called him "the unseen general,"[33] hinting that he relayed the words of God from heaven to influence events on earth. His "army" was not a massed military, but the peaceful reign of God.

Cardinal Sin was later asked about his political involvement and said simply that he wanted to add a "moral dimension"[34] to the social arena.

Placed in the cauldron of suffering and oppression, Cardinal Sin courageously stood by God's moral dimension. The "unseen general" encouraged the people to stand together for their own dignity and their quest for liberation. Then-president of Santa Clara University Rev. Paul L. Locatelli noted, "If you compare him to Romero, he spoke out as much as Romero did.…He saw justice as making sure that the poor had a voice."[35]

NOTES

INTRODUCTION

1. Marie Paul Curley and Madonna Therese Radliff, eds., *Bread of Life: Prayers for Eucharistic Adoration* (Boston: Pauline Books and Media, 2004), 20.

2. Augustine, *The City of God*, trans. Marcus Dods (New York: Random House, 1993), 310.

3. *The Liturgy of the Hours*, vol. 2: *Lenten Season, Easter Season* (New York: Catholic Book Publishing, 1976), 653.

PART I

1. "Building to Be Renamed for Pioneer Black Educator Anne Marie Becraft," Georgetown University: News, accessed June 1, 2023, https://www.georgetown.edu/news/building-to-be-renamed-for-pioneer-black-educator-anne-marie-becraft/.

2. Georgetown University, "Building to Be Renamed."

3. Shannen Dee Williams, *Subversive Habits: Black Catholic Nuns and the Long African American Freedom Struggle* (Durham, NC: Duke University Press, 2022), 30.

4. Georgetown University, "Building to Be Renamed."

5. Charlene Smith and John Feister, *Thea's Song: The Life of Thea Bowman* (Maryknoll, NY: Orbis Books, 2009), 179.

6. Smith and Feister, *Thea's Song*, 100–101.

7. Smith and Feister, *Thea's Song*, 207.

8. Smith and Feister, *Thea's Song*, 260.

9. Smith and Feister, *Thea's Song*, 261.

10. See this powerful moment at https://www.youtube.com/watch?v=uOV0nQkjuoA.

11. Smith and Feister, *Thea's Song*, 200.

12. "Thea Bowman in Her Own Words," Spirituality and Practice: Book Reviews, accessed June 1, 2023, https://www.spiritualityandpractice.com/book-reviews/view/18810/thea-bowman.

13. Campbell, Simone, *A Nun on the Bus: How All of Us Can Create Hope, Change and Community* (New York: HarperOne, 2014), 6.

14. Campbell, *Nun on the Bus*, 13.

15. Campbell, *Nun on the Bus*, xiv.

16. Dan Stockman, "Sr. Simone Campbell, Spirit Will Lead the Way," *National Catholic Reporter*, April 2–15, 2021, 1.

17. Campbell, *Nun on the Bus*, 93.

18. Campbell, *Nun on the Bus*, 109.

19. Stockman, "Sr. Simone Campbell," 6.

20. Stockman, "Sr. Simone Campbell," 6.

21. Campbell, *Nun on the Bus*, xii.

22. Anita Caspary, *Witness to Integrity: The Crisis of the Immaculate Heart of Mary Community of California* (Collegeville, MN: Liturgical Press, 2003), 19.

23. Caspary, *Witness to Integrity*, 1.

24. Caspary, *Witness to Integrity*, xiii.

25. Caspary, *Witness to Integrity*, 269.

26. John of the Cross, *The Collected Works of St. John of the Cross*, trans. Kieran Kavanaugh and Otilio Rodriquez (Washington, DC: ICS Publications, 1991), 615.

27. Caspary, *Witness to Integrity*, 219.

28. Williams, *Subversive Habits*, 2.

29. Williams, *Subversive Habits*, 158.

30. Williams, *Subversive Habits*, 2.

31. Williams, *Subversive Habits*, 135.

32. Williams, *Subversive Habits*, 134.

33. Williams, *Subversive Habits*, 4.

34. "Franciscan Sr. Mary Antona Ebo, Civil Rights Leader, Dies at 93," *Global Sisters Report*, accessed April 13, 2023, https://www.globalsistersreport.org/news/ministry/franciscan-sr-mary-antona-ebo-civil-rights-leader-dies-93-50376.

35. "Sister Mary Antona Ebo," Adrian Dominican Sisters: Equity and Inclusion, accessed June 22, 2023, https://adriandominicans.org/Equity-and-Inclusion/sister-mary-antona-ebo-fsm-1924-2017.

36. Williams, *Subversive Habits*, 154.

37. Williams, *Subversive Habits*, 175.

38. Williams, *Subversive Habits*, 175.

39. Williams, *Subversive Habits*, 176.

40. Williams, *Subversive Habits*, 177.

41. Williams, *Subversive Habits*, 185.

42. Williams, *Subversive Habits*, 185.

43. "Black Sisters Group Takes Archbishop to Task for Comments on Social Justice," *Global Sisters Report*: News, accessed March 1, 2023, https://www.globalsistersreport.org/news/news/news/black-sisters-group-takes-archbishop-task-comments-social-justice.

44. Williams, *Subversive Habits*, Survival of Soul Document, 1970, National Black Sisters Conference, 197.

45. "Transforming Lives Impacted by Crime through Healing Services and Relationships," Restorative Partners, accessed March 3, 2023, https://restorativepartners.org/.

46. Theresa Harpin, phone interview with author, April 6, 2023. Unless otherwise noted in this section, all quotes and information are from this interview.

47. Francis Evans, ed., *New Saint Joseph's People's Prayer Book* (New York: Catholic Book Publishing, 1993), 430.

48. Restorative Partners, accessed March 3, 2023, https://restorativepartners.org/.

49. Eduardo Campos Lima, "A Franciscan Sister Joins the Fight for Indigenous Rights in Brazil," *America*, October 14, 2021, https://www.americamagazine.org/politics-society/2021/10/14/laura-manso-franciscan-sister-indigenous-rights-brazil-territory-lumber.

50. Pilar Timpane, "In the Amazon, Religious Women Lead the Way," *The Revealer*, March 7, 2023, https://therevealer.org/in-the-amazon-religious-women-lead-the-way/.

51. Lise Alves, "Sisters Help Brazil's Indigenous with Land Rights, Identity and Survival," *Global Sisters Report*, April 17, 2023, https://www.globalsistersreport.org/news/sisters-help-brazils-indigenous-land-rights-identity-and-survival-0.

52. Alves, "Sisters Help Brazil's Indigenous."

53. Alves, "Sisters Help Brazil's Indigenous."

54. Timpane, "In the Amazon."

55. James T. Keane, "The Four Martyred Churchwomen Dare Us to Be Saints," *America*, December 6, 2022, https://www.americamagazine.org/arts-culture/2022/12/06/martyrs-churchwomen-salvador-anniversary-244279.

56. Maryknoll Lay Missioners, "Jean Donovan, Lay Missioner Martyred in 1980," November 6, 2020, accessed May 12, 2023, https://mklm.org/el-salvador/jean-donovan-lay-missioner-martyred-in-1980/.

57. Maryknoll Sisters, "Sister Ita Ford," accessed March 13, 2023, https://www.maryknollsisters.org/40thanniversary/sister-ita-ford-2/.

58. Maryknoll Sisters, "Sister Maura Clarke," accessed March 13, 2023, https://www.maryknollsisters.org/40thanniversary/sister-maura-clarke-2/.

59. Maryknoll Sisters, "Sister Maura Clarke."

60. "Sister Dorothy Kazel," Ursulines of the Roman Union, accessed March 13, 2023, https://ursulines-roman-union.org/en/sister-dorothy-kazel.

61. Maryknoll Lay Missioners, "Jean Donovan."

62. Maryknoll Lay Missioners, "Jean Donovan."

63. Maryknoll Sisters, "Ita Ford."

64. Karl Rahner, *Theological Investigations*, vol. 8: *Further Theology of the Spiritual Life 2* (New York: Seabury, 1977), 88.

65. Ecclesia of Women in Asia, accessed December 29, 2023, https://ecclesiaofwomenblog.wordpress.com/.

66. Ecclesia of Women in Asia, "Home Page."

67. Ecclesia of Women in Asia, "About EWA," video.

68. Ecclesia of Women in Asia, "Bangkok 2002, Closing Liturgy," accessed December 29, 2023, https://ecclesiaofwomenblog.wordpress.com/2017/04/18/ewa1closingliturgy/.

69. Ecclesia of Women in Asia, "Closing Liturgy."

70. Ecclesia of Women in Asia, "About EWA."

71. Carol Zimmerman, "Sister Norma Pimentel Is One of Time Magazine's 100 Most Influential People of 2020," *Global Sisters Report*: News, September 23, 2020, https://www.globalsistersreport.org/news/sr-norma-pimentel-one-time-magazines-100-most-influential-people-2020.

72. Zimmerman, "Sister Norma Pimentel."

73. Zimmerman, "Sister Norma Pimental."

74. Norma Pimentel, "The Border Crisis in the Rio Grande Valley," TED, accessed March 5, 2023, https://www.ted.com/talks/sister_norma_pimentel_the_border_crisis_in_the_rio_grande_valley.

75. Pimentel, "Border Crisis."

76. Helen Prejean, *River of Fire: My Spiritual Journey* (New York: Random House, 2019), 282.

77. Prejean, *River of Fire*, xv.

78. Prejean, *River of Fire*, 23–24.

79. "Pope John's Opening Speech to the Council," Vatican II, Voice of the Church, accessed April 2, 2023, https://vatican2voice.org/91docs/opening_speech.htm.

80. Prejean, *River of Fire*, 104.

81. Prejean, *River of Fire*, 241.
82. Prejean, *River of Fire*, 243–44.
83. Prejean, *River of Fire*, 252.
84. Prejean, *River of Fire*, 253.
85. John of the Cross, *The Collected Works*, 90.

PART II

1. "Biography of Marguerite Barankitse, African Solidarity," Salient Women: Biographies of Extraordinary Women, accessed March 13, 2023, https://www.salientwomen.com/2020/10/12/biography-of-marguerite-barankitse-african-solidarity/.

2. Georgetown University: Berkeley Center for Religion, Peace and World Affairs, "A Discussion with Marguerite Barankitse, Maison Shalom, Burundi," accessed April 1, 2023, https://berkleycenter.georgetown.edu/interviews/a-discussion-with-marguerite-barankitse-maison-shalom-burundi.

3. Georgetown University, "A Discussion with Marguerite Barankitse."

4. Nobel Women's Initiative, "Meet Marguerite Barankitse, Burundi," accessed April 2, 2023, https://www.nobelwomensinitiative.org/meet-marguerite-barankitse-burundi.

5. Nobel Women's Initiative, "Meet Marguerite Barankitse."

6. Boston College: BC News, "Celebrating Copeland," accessed March 15, 2023, https://www.bc.edu/bc-web/bcnews/faith-religion/theology/copeland-retirement.html.

7. M. Shawn Copeland, *Knowing Christ Crucified: The Witness of African-American Religious Experience* (Maryknoll, NY: Orbis Books, 2018), xiii.

8. Copeland, *Knowing Christ Crucified*, xxiii.

9. Copeland, *Knowing Christ Crucified*, xxiv.

10. Copeland, *Knowing Christ Crucified*, xxiv.

11. Copeland, *Knowing Christ Crucified*, xxiv.

12. Copeland, *Knowing Christ Crucified*, xi.

13. Boston College, "Celebrating Copeland."

14. Changing the Face of Medicine, "Dr. Lena Francis Edwards," accessed January 15, 2023, https://cfmedicine.nlm.nih.gov/physicians/biography_96.html.

15. Changing the Face of Medicine, "Dr. Lena Francis Edwards."

16. Changing the Face of Medicine, "Dr. Lena Francis Edwards."

17. Changing the Face of Medicine, "Dr. Lena Francis Edwards."

18. New Jersey Women's History, "Lena Frances Edwards," accessed January 14, 2023, https://njwomenshistory.org/biographies/lena-frances-edwards/.

19. John Dear, "Paul Farmer: Saint with a Stethoscope," *America*, April 2022, 10.

20. Partners In Health, "Mission," accessed March 2, 2023, https://www.pih.org/our-mission.

21. Partners In Health, "Injustice Has a Cure," accessed March 2, 2023, https://www.pih.org/.

22. Dear, "Paul Farmer," 10.

23. Dear, "Paul Farmer," 10.

24. Michael Griffin and Jennie Weiss Block, eds., *In the Company of the Poor: Conversations with Dr. Paul Farmer and Fr. Gustavo Gutierrez* (Maryknoll, NY: Orbis Books 2013), 3.

25. Griffin and Block, *In the Company of the Poor*, 4.

26. Dear, "Paul Farmer," 10.

27. Paul Farmer, *To Repair the World: Paul Farmer Speaks to the Next Generation*, ed. Jonathan Wiegel (Oakland: University of California Press, 2013), 212.

28. "Burke Lecture, Dr. Elisabeth Schussler Fiorenza," UCTV: Great Minds Gather Here, University of California Television, https://www.uctv.tv/shows/Burke-Lecture-Elizabeth-Schussler-Fiorenza-12211.

29. Fiorenza, "Burke Lecture."

30. Oblate School of Theology, Sankofa Institute, "Standing in the Shoes My Mother Made, Diana Hayes," https://ost.edu/standing-shoes-mother-made/.

31. Oblate School of Theology, "Diana Hayes."

32. "Breaking Barriers," *America*, July 7–14, 2014, https://www.americamagazine.org/issue/culture/breaking-barriers.

33. "Breaking Barriers."

34. Dolores R. Leckey and Kathleen Dolphin, eds., *Monika Hellwig: The People's Theologian* (Collegeville, MN: Liturgical Press, 2010), 8.

35. Leo J. Donovan, "The Vocation of a Theologian," *America*, November 28, 2005, https://www.americamagazine.org/issue/552/faith-focus/vocation-theologian.

36. "Proceedings of the Catholic Theological Society of America," Boston College, https://ejournals.bc.edu/index.php/ctsa/article/view/3432/3033.

37. Leckey and Dolphin, *Monika Hellwig*, 54.

38. Donovan, "The Vocation of a Theologian."

39. Jacques Maritain, *The Person and the Common Good* (Notre Dame, IN: University of Notre Dame Press, 1966), 26.

40. Maritain, *The Person and the Common Good*, 53.

41. Maritain, *The Person and the Common Good*, 85.

42. Maritain, *The Person and the Common Good*, 42.

43. Juvenalis R. Paulo Baitu, *Mwalimu Julius Kambarage Nyerere's Vision of Education* (Bukoba, Tanzania: Tanzania Educational Publisher, 2019), 13.

44. Marissa Evans, "(1967) The Arusha Declaration," The BlackPast: Global African History, August 9, 2012, https://www

.blackpast.org/global-african-history/arusha-declaration-1967-2/#:~:text=The%20Arusha%20Declaration%2C%20which%20was,Tanzania%20between%201964%20and%201985.

45. Baitu, *Mwalimu Julius Kambarage Nyerere's Vision*, 33–34.

46. Baitu, *Mwalimu Julius Kambarage Nyerere's Vision*, 66.

47. Julius K. Nyerere, *Man and Development: Binadamu Na Maendeleo* (London: Oxford University Press, 1974), 91, 98.

48. Peter F. O'Brien, "Jazz for the Soul," Liner Notes for *Mary Lou Williams: Presents Black Christ of the Andes*, recorded between August 1962 and November 1963, Smithsonian Folkways Recordings, 2004, SFW CD 40816, page 8.

49. Eddie Meadows, "Foreward" [*sic*], liner notes for *Mary Lou Williams: Presents Black Christ of the Andes*, recorded between August 1962 and November 1963, Smithsonian Folkways Recordings, 2004, SFW CD 40816, page 2.

50. O'Brien, "Jazz for the Soul," 10–11.

51. O'Brien, "Jazz for the Soul," 9.

PART III

1. Kevin F. Burke, ed., *Pedro Arrupe: Essential Writings* (Maryknoll, NY: Orbis Books 2004), 201.

2. Burke, *Pedro Arrupe*, 196–97.

3. Burke, *Pedro Arrupe*, 24.

4. Pedro Arrupe, *In Him Alone Is Our Hope: Texts on the Heart of Christ* (Chestnut Hill, MA: Institute of Jesuit Studies, 2021), 69.

5. Daniel Berrigan, *The Nightmare of God: The Book of Revelation* (Eugene, OR: Wipf and Stock, 2009), 106.

6. Daniel Lewis, "Daniel J. Berrigan, Defiant Priest Who Preached Pacifism, Dies at 94," *New York Times*, April 30, 2016, https://www.nytimes.com/2016/05/01/nyregion/

daniel-j-berrigan-defiant-priest-who-preached-pacifism-dies-at-94.html.

7. Robert F. Burke and Robert Lassalle-Klein, eds., *Love That Produces Hope: The Thought of Ignacio Ellacuría* (Collegeville, MN: Liturgical Press, 2006), xiii.

8. Britannica, "Xavier Zubiri, Spanish Philosopher," https://www.britannica.com/biography/Xavier-Zubiri#ref1044217.

9. Burke and Lassalle-Klein, *Love That Produces Hope*, 174–75.

10. J. Mathew Ashley, Kevin Burke, and Rodolfo Cardenal, eds., *A Grammar of Justice: The Legacy of Ignacio Ellacuría* (Maryknoll, NY: Orbis Books, 2014), 37.

11. Ignacio Ellacuría and Michael Lee, ed., *Ignacio Ellacuría: Essays on History, Liberation, and Salvation* (Maryknoll, NY: Orbis Books, 2013), 58.

12. Thomas Kelly, *When the Gospel Grows Feet: An Ecclesiology in Context* (Collegeville, MN: Liturgical Press), 86.

13. Kelly, *When the Gospel Grows Feet*, 85–86.

14. Kelly, *When the Gospel Grows Feet*, 163.

15. Kelly, *When the Gospel Grows Feet*, 214–15.

16. Kelly, *When the Gospel Grows Feet*, xiv.

17. Bernard Häring, *Free and Faithful: My Life in the Catholic Church* (Ligouri, MO: Ligouri/Triumph, 1998), 8.

18. Bernard Häring, *The Law of Christ: Moral Theology for Priests and Laity* (Paramus, NJ: Newman Press, 1966), dust jacket of hardcover edition.

19. Häring, *The Law of Christ*, 35.

20. Häring, *The Law of Christ*, 36.

21. Häring, *The Law of Christ*, 37–38.

22. Häring, *Free and Faithful*, 95.

23. Häring, *Free and Faithful*, 79.

24. Hans Küng, *My Struggle for Freedom: Memoirs* (Grand Rapids, MI: Eerdmans, 2003), 305.

25. Küng, *My Struggle for Freedom*, 306.

26. Küng, *My Struggle for Freedom*, 64.

27. Hans Küng, *The Church Maintained in Truth: A Theological Meditation* (New York: Random House, 1982), 67.

28. Küng, *The Church Maintained in Truth*, 36.

29. Küng, *The Church Maintained in Truth*, 22–25.

30. Bernard Lonergan, *Method in Theology* (Toronto: University of Toronto Press, 1971), 5.

31. Lonergan, *Method in Theology*, 44–45.

32. Lonergan, *Method in Theology*, 55.

33. Lonergan, *Method in Theology*, 105–6.

34. Lonergan, *Method in Theology*, 111.

35. Lonergan, *Method in Theology*, 117.

36. Lonergan, *Method in Theology*, 117–18.

37. Boston College: The Lonergan Institute, "About Bernard Lonergan SJ," accessed March 12, 2023, https://www.bc.edu/bc-web/academics/sites/the-lonergan-institute/about/about-lonergan.html.

38. Lonergan, *Method in Theology*, 119.

39. Lonergan, *Method in Theology*, 119.

40. Martin Ott, "Engelbert Mveng, A Sword Will Pierce Your Own Heart Also. An African Pieta," VCS: The Visual Commentary on Scripture, accessed March 10, 2023, https://thevcs.org/sword-will-pierce-your-own-heart-also/african-pieta.

41. Ott, "Englebert Mveng, An African Pieta."

42. Akintunde E. Akinade, "The Crucible of Faith: Justice and Liberation in the Work of Engelbert Mveng," *QScience*: Hamad Bin Khalifa University Press, https://www.qscience.com/content/journals/10.5339/rels.2012.justice.17.

43. Akinade, "The Crucible of Faith."

44. Akinade, "The Crucible of Faith."

45. Caroline Hemesath, *From Slave to Priest: The Inspirational Story of Father Augustine Tolton (1854–1897)* (San Francisco: Ignatius Press, 2006), 108–9.

46. Hemesath, *From Slave to Priest*, 102.

47. Hemesath, *From Slave to Priest*, 102.

48. Hemesath, *From Slave to Priest*, 203.

49. Hemesath, *From Slave to Priest*, 185.

50. Hemesath, *From Slave to Priest*, 117.

PART IV

1. Richard Sandomir, "Cardinal Paulo Evaristo Arns Dies at 95; Fought Torture in Brazil," *New York Times*, December 18, 2016, https://www.nytimes.com/2016/12/18/world/americas/cardinal-paulo-evaristo-arns-brazil-dead.html.

2. Peter Stanford, "Cardinal Paulo Evaristo Arns Obituary," *Guardian*, December 16, 2016, https://www.theguardian.com/world/2016/dec/16/cardinal-paulo-everisto-arns-obituary.

3. Lise Alves, "Brazilian Cardinal Arns, 95, Remembered for His Fight for Human Rights," *National Catholic Reporter*, December 16, 2016, https://www.ncronline.org/brazilian-cardinal-arns-95-remembered-his-fight-human-rights.

4. Stanford, "Cardinal Paulo Evaristo Arns."

5. Sandomir, "Cardinal Evaristo Arns Dies at 95."

6. Sandomir, "Cardinal Evaristo Arns Dies at 95."

7. Matthew Fox, *The Pope's War: Why Ratzinger's Secret Crusade Has Imperiled the Church and How It Can Be Saved* (New York: Sterling Ethos, 2011), 54.

8. Fox, *The Pope's War*, 55.

9. Lise Alves, "Pedro Casaldáliga, Bishop of the Poor, Dies in Brazil at 92," Earthbeat: A Project of *National Catho-*

lic Reporter, https://www.ncronline.org/earthbeat/politics/pedro-casald-liga-bishop-poor-dies-brazil-92.

10. Fox, *The Pope's War,* 61.

11. Fox, *The Pope's War,* 60.

12. Alves, "Pedro Casadáliga."

13. Alves, "Pedro Casadáliga."

14. Sean Salai, "Bishop Thomas Gumbleton: War Isn't the Solution to Our Problems," *America,* November 18, 2015, https://www.americamagazine.org/content/all-things/social-justice-all-interview-bishop-thomas-gumbleton.

15. "No Guilty Bystander; The Extraordinary Life and Times of Catholic Bishop Thomas Gumbleton of Detroit," Religion News Service, June 22, 2023, https://religionnews.com/2023/06/22/no-guilty-bystander/.

16. United States Conference of Catholic Bishops (USCCB), "The Challenge of Peace: God's Promise and Our Response," May 3, 1983, 58, https://www.usccb.org/upload/challenge-peace-gods-promise-our-response-1983.pdf.

17. USCCB, "The Challenge of Peace," 333.

18. Aleja Hertzler-McCain, "Bishop Gumbleton Reflects on Past, Present and Future of Pax Christi USA," *National Catholic Reporter,* August 2, 2022, https://www.ncronline.org/news/people/bishop-gumbleton-reflects-past-future-pax-christi-usa.

19. Hertzler-McCain, "Bishop Gumbleton."

20. Thomas Gumbleton, "The Solemnity of the Most Holy Body and Blood of Christ (Corpus Christi)," *National Catholic Reporter,* June 23, 2006, https://www.ncronline.org/blogs/peace-pulpit/solemnity-most-holy-body-and-blood-christ-corpus-christi.

21. John A. McCoy, *A Still and Quiet Conscience: The Archbishop Who Challenged a Pope, a President and a Church; A Life of Raymond G. Hunthausen* (Maryknoll, NY: Orbis Books, 2015), 105.

22. McCoy, *A Still and Quiet Conscience*, 105.

23. McCoy, *A Still and Quiet Conscience*, 105.

24. McCoy, *A Still and Quiet Conscience*, 39.

25. McCoy, *A Still and Quiet Conscience*, 176.

26. McCoy, *A Still and Quiet Conscience*, 293.

27. McCoy, *A Still and Quiet Conscience*, 293.

28. Adam Easton, "Obituary: Cardinal Jaime Sin," June 21, 2005, *Guardian*, https://www.theguardian.com/news/2005/jun/22/guardianobituaries.world.

29. Easton, "Obituary: Cardinal Jaime Sin."

30. "Benigno "Ninoy" Aquino Jr.," Harvard Divinity School: Religion and Public Life, accessed December 29, 2023, https://rpl.hds.harvard.edu/faq/benigno-%E2%80%9Cninoy%E2%80%9D-aquino-jr.

31. Easton, "Obituary: Cardinal Jaime Sin."

32. "People Power," Harvard Divinity School: Religion and Public Life, accessed December 29, 2023, https://rpl.hds.harvard.edu/faq/people-power.

33. Michelle O'Donnell, "Cardinal Jaime Sin, a Champion of the Poor in the Philippines, Is Dead at 76," June 21, 2005, https://www.nytimes.com/2005/06/21/obituaries/cardinal-jaime-sin-a-champion-of-the-poor-in-the-philippines-is.html.

34. O'Donnell, "Cardinal Sin."

35. O'Donnell, "Cardinal Sin."

SELECTED BIBLIOGRAPHY

Arrupe, Pedro. *In Him Alone Is Our Hope: Texts on the Heart of Christ*. Chestnut Hill, MA: Institute of Jesuit Studies, 2021.

Ashley, Matthew J., Kevin F. Burke, and Rodolfo Cardenal, eds. *A Grammar of Justice: The Legacy of Ignacio Ellacuría*. Maryknoll, NY: Orbis Books, 2014.

Augustine. *The City of God*. Translated by Marcus Dods. New York: Random House, Modern Library Edition, 1993.

Baitu, Juvenalis R. Paulo. *Mwalimu Julius Kambarage Nyerere's Vision of Education*. Bukoba, Tanzania: Tanzania Educational Publishers, 2019.

Berrigan, Daniel. *The Nightmare of God: The Book of Revelation*. Eugene, OR: Wipf and Stock, 2009.

Burke, Kevin F. *Pedro Arrupe: Essential Writings*. Maryknoll, NY: Orbis Books, 2004.

Campbell, Simone. *A Nun on the Bus: How All of Us Can Create Hope, Change and Community*. New York: HarperOne, 2014.

Chachage, Chambi, and Annar Cassam. *Africa's Liberation: The Legacy of Julius Nyerere*. Cape Town, South Africa: Pambazuka Press, 2010.

Copeland, M. Shawn. *Knowing Christ Crucified: The Witness of African American Religious Experience*. Maryknoll, NY: Orbis Books, 2018.

Crowe, Frederick E., and Robert M. Doran, ed. *The Collected Works of Bernard Lonergan*. Vol. 3: *Insight: A Study of*

Human Understanding. Toronto: University of Toronto Press 1992.

Davis, Cyprian. *A History of Black Catholics in the United States*. New York: Crossroad, 2004.

Evans, Francis. *New Saint Joseph People's Prayer Book*. New York: Catholic Publishing, 1993.

Farmer, Paul. *To Repair the World: Paul Farmer Speaks to the Next Generation*. Edited by Jonathan Weigel. Oakland: University of California Press, 2013.

Fiorenza, Elisabeth Schüssler. *Jesus: Miriam's Child, Sophia's Prophet: Critical Issues in Feminist Christology*. London: Bloomsbury T & T Clark, 2015.

———. *The Power of the Word: Scripture and the Rhetoric of Empire*. Minneapolis: Fortress, 2007.

Flannery, Austin, ed. *The Basic Sixteen Documents: Vatican II Council, Constitutions, Decrees, Declarations*. Northport, NY: Costello, 1996.

Fox, Matthew. *The Pope's War: Why Ratzinger's Secret Crusade Has Imperiled the Church and How It Can Be Saved*. New York: Sterling Ethos, 2011.

Grigsby, Daryl. *In Their Footsteps: Inspirational Reflections on Black History for Every Day of the Year*. Skokie, IL: Acta Publications, 2007.

Häring, Bernard. *Free and Faithful: My Life in the Catholic Church*. Ligouri, MO: Ligouri Triumph, 1998.

———. *The Law of Christ: Moral Theology for Priests and Laity*. Paramus, NJ: Newman Press, 1966.

Hayes, Diana, and Cyprian Davis. *Taking Down Our Harps: Black Catholics in the United States*. Maryknoll, NY: Orbis Books, 1998.

Hemesath, Caroline. *From Slave to Priest: A Biography of the Reverend Augustine Tolton (1854–1897); The First Black Priest of the United States*. San Francisco: Ignatius, 2006.

Kelly, Thomas M. *When the Gospel Grows Feet: An Ecclesiology in Context*. Collegeville, MN: Liturgical Press, 2013.

Küng, Hans. *Can We Save the Catholic Church?* London: William Collins, 2013.

———. *The Church*. London: Burns & Oates, 2013.

———. *The Church Maintained in Truth*. New York: Random House, 1982.

———. *My Struggle for Freedom: Memoirs*. Grand Rapids, MI, Canada: Eerdmans, 2003.

Leckey, Dolores R., and Kathleen Dolphin. *Monika Hellwig: The People's Theologian*. Collegeville, MN: Liturgical Press, 2010.

Lee, Michael, ed. *Ignacio Ellacuría: Essays on History, Liberation and Salvation*. Maryknoll, NY: Orbis Books, 2013.

Logan, Rayford. *The Betrayal of the Negro: From Rutherford B. Hayes to Woodrow Wilson*. New York: Da Capo Press, 1997.

Lonergan, Bernard. *Method in Theology*. Toronto: University of Toronto Press, 1971.

Maritain, Jacques. *An Introduction to Philosophy*. London: Continuum, 2005.

———. *The Person and the Common Good*. Notre Dame, IN: University of Notre Dame Press, 1966.

McCoy, John A. *A Still and Quiet Conscience: The Archbishop Who Challenged a Pope, a President, and a Church; A Life of Raymond G. Hunthausen*. Maryknoll, NY: Orbis Books, 2015.

Nyerere, Julius K. *Man and Development; Binadamu Na Maendelelo*. London: Oxford University Press, 1974.

O'Brien, David J., and Thomas A. Shannon. *Catholic Social Thought: The Documentary Heritage*. Maryknoll, NY: Orbis Books, 2010.

Rahner, Karl. *Theological Investigations*, vol. 8: *Further Theology of the Spiritual Life 2*. New York, Seabury, 1977.

Smith, Charlene, and John Feister. *Thea's Song: The Life of Thea Bowman*. Maryknoll, NY: Orbis Books, 2009.

Williams, Shannen Dee. *Subversive Habits: Black Catholic Nuns in the Long African American Freedom Struggle*. Durham, NC: Duke University Press, 2022.